The
HISTORY
and GROWTH *of*
CHURCHES
of CHRIST *in*
NIGERIA,
1948–2000

ENO O. OTOYO, Ed.D

THE HISTORY AND GROWTH OF CHURCHES OF CHRIST IN NIGERIA, 1948–2000

iUniverse books may be ordered through booksellers or by contacting:

iUniverse
1663 Liberty Drive
Bloomington, IN 47403
www.iuniverse.com
844-349-9409

All scripture references in this book are from the New International Version of the Holy Bible.

ISBN: 978-1-6632-1898-8 (sc)
ISBN: 978-1-6632-1899-5 (e)

Library of Congress Control Number: 2021909686

Print information available on the last page.

iUniverse rev. date: 05/28/2021

CONTENTS

PREFACE

Prior to the establishment of the Church of Christ in 1948, Nigeria had multiple churches with diverse teachings and practices. Between 1948 and 2000, the period this book covers, evangelistic activism and expansion of the Church of Christ saw the church spreading into many villages, towns, and cities. By this time, people had grown disenchanted with some of the prevailing teachings. Flocks of denominational members, who desired to know what the Bible teaches on various biblical subjects, felt they were denied or given unsatisfactory answers.

To remain faithful and active in their respective churches, those who wanted schools and hospitals began to question and agitate, as though the requirements for admission into their institutions were requisites for righteousness and entry into heaven. Some felt ignored or treated unfairly by their organizational hierarchy. They grew impatient over what they perceived as lack of concern and indifference.

There were conflicting voices and practices, in opposition to Christ's provision in the scriptures, as the basis for unity, doctrine, and Christian observance. The diversity in hermeneutical views and practices among religious denominations appeared to have defied Christ's dictum that Christians should speak the same thing and be perfectly joined in the same mind and the same judgment.

This book will present the historical events, the motivation, and the inspiration that energized the establishment and rapid growth of the Church of Christ in Nigeria. Most organizations' histories are built around specific events, and they provide a timeline in which certain events transpired. Believers and curiosity seekers cherish how a group or organization came into existence. The direction and the sacrifices made to preserve the system or organization have, in many cases, been documented for posterity and for the larger community to append their sanction on the merits of such an organization.

In every organization, including church groups, there is a leader with ingenuity and intuitive insight whom followers have seen fit to embrace. Such a history usually is not easy to narrate, especially when the chronicler claims to have participated actively in the events portrayed. The temptation to exaggerate and emote often clouds the writer's perception and misleads readers. The essence of accurate chronology is the factual documentation of the unfolding events and information, not hearsay speculations. It is pertinent that I witnessed and actively participated in the unfolding events and that I accurately traced and documented for posterity, without exaggeration, the advent and basic doctrines of the church in Nigeria. I also researched by consulting past and current American missionaries serving in Nigeria with local national evangelists, and I visited over thirty local churches.

The restoration movement, unlike the reformation movement, seeks not to reform or develop a theology of retreading God's words but accepting God's authoritative injunctions and rules as from God, not human beings. This issue is the point of divergence between God's mandate and humans' continuous search to change and adapt God's words to their changing views.

The restoration movement by Churches of Christ is pleading for reconsideration of the concept of and belief in original sin, especially in the doctrine involving the teachings and practices of baptizing children because they, by nature, have inherited their fathers' sins.

Another area of great concern with the restoration movement is that of organizational structure and governance of the church. Is it conceivable that God would establish his kingdom and leave it in human hands, without a barometer, structure, or strategic plan for governance? From the Old Testament through the New Testament, God specifically instituted a theological compass of governance for his people. The apostle Paul, through the Holy Spirit, intuited,

> "What does he ascended mean except that
> he also descended to the lower, earthly
> regions? He who descended is the very

one who ascended higher than all the heavens, to fill the whole universe. It was he who gave some to be apostles. Some to be prophets, some to be evangelists, and some to be pastors and teachers, to prepare God's people for works of service, so that the body of Christ may be built up until we all reach unity in the faith and in the knowledge of the Son of God and become mature, attaining to the whole measure of the fullness of Christ."[1]

God certainly has a plan for the day-to-day roles and management of his subjects.

There are numerous other issues, such as the purpose of baptism, which is a burial:

Don't you know that all of us who were baptized into Christ Jesus were baptized into his death? We were therefore buried with him through baptism into death in order that, just as Christ was raised from the dead through the glory of the Father, we too may live a new life.[2]

Luke, the author of Acts of the Apostles, states, "Repent and be baptized every one of you in the name of Jesus Christ for the remission of sins."[3]

Saint Paul, commenting on the financial support for the church, stipulates, "On the first day of the week each one of you should lay aside a sum of money in keeping with his income, saving it up so that when I come no collection will have to be made."[4] Paul writing to Titus wrote, "The reason I left you in Crete was that you might straighten out what was left unfinished and appoint elders in every town."[5]

Qualifications for the ordination of leaders, elders, presbyters, bishops and/or overseers are titles that are used synonymously. For example, in Acts 20:28, Paul summoned the elders at Ephesus for a conference in which he warned that they keep watch over themselves and all the flock of which the Holy Spirit has made you (them) overseers, (Verse 28). Elders and overseers are interchangeable. Again, these titles were synonymously applied, based on biblical qualifications, not on human standards. Whichever title a congregation or groups of congregations decides to use or wear, does not elevate one over the others. Every member was and is called a *saint*, not a select person or group of people. Don't you know that the saints will judge the world? 1Cor. 6:2; any person who appropriates to himself or is conferred a "saint" as a special title above pew members, contradicts the scriptures.

I offer my deep gratitude to those who shared their insight—evangelists, church members, and missionaries who responded to the survey sent from 1987 to 2008. Many of the respondents took a much longer time to return their responses because of adverse and communication problems; it was impractical to establish a cut-off time for the collection of responses. From the responses, many of the facts have been documented and collated. Men like Etim Asuquo at Surulere Church of Christ in Lagos; Etim Robert Offiong of Stadium Road Church of Christ, Oron; Brother Howard Horton; Bill Curry; and Ita Johnson at Calabar contributed immensely.

In this process, there were regions, towns, cities, and villages that were not covered. Unfortunately, deficient statistical information from other churches is attributed to lack of communication, unavailability of records, or unresponsiveness from desired sources. Nonetheless, the wealth of information collected represents the position and teaching of the church. Perhaps future generations will recognize the need and importance of sharing information that will enhance better documentation of historical events for posterity.

ACKNOWLEDGMENTS

This book could not have been accomplished without the many contributions and a wealth of data gathered from various individuals, such as Brother Etim Asuquo, a first-year colleague of the Bible Training College, Ukpom, Abak, who provided answers relative to the work at Lagos and his early knowledge and contact with Coolidge Akpan Okon (C. A. O.) Essien, whom he met and knew intimately. Solomon U. U. Etuk was my partner in tribulation while we served among fifty-three congregations in Itu and Ibiono. Brother George Ekong Sr., one of the patriarchs of our faith in Nigeria and a pioneer minister who was taught by Brother C. A. O. Essien, was incredibly helpful. He authorized his written speeches on the history of the church, to be used in any way that related to further theses on the church.

I had the good fortune of receiving useful information from Brother Ita Effiong Johnson, an alumnus, who later became the principal of the Christian Technical College, Oyubia Town, Oron, on the work in Calabar, including the regions beyond. There were men like Howard Horton, my mentor, who was with Jimmy Johnson as the first Church of Christ missionaries to arrive in Nigeria in 1952. He was instrumental in verifying and attesting to facts that occurred during his years of service. Brother

Elvis Huffard and Reese Bryant provided scrupulously documented data on the administration of the Christian elementary schools that were impressive and helpful. Dr. Henry Farrar, the brains behind the establishment and the administrator of the Nigerian Christian Hospital, Onicha Ngwa, graciously provided a wealth of documents, with volumes of pictures of the patients treated at the hospital.

Brother Douglas and Sister Scharla Lawyer accommodated us in their home when, from the road through Asaba to Oron, we had a terrible car accident two days after we arrived in Nigeria. Brother Lawyer was a serious, mindful person who was jovial yet dedicated to his work and who kept us titillated with old spurn jokes, jokes that have been bantered for years. These were people of immeasurably encouraging dispositions.

Brother John Whitney, the son-in-law of Brother Francis F. Carson, and his wife, Carol, were instrumental in providing original communications between Carson and Ukpekpe, a man who was engrossed in the creation of the First Negro Church of Christ. John is to be commended for his open-heartedness and willingness to share Carson's valuable records.

My gratitude goes to Mr. Ubon Udoh, who, under difficult circumstances, persevered to provide me with useful computerized information. Christopher Bischel served as my computer consultant, troubleshooting whenever my knowledge of computers was ineffectual.

To my ever-abiding, loving wife, LaVera Eugene (Hamilton) Otoyo.

She took a leap in the dark, adventured into Africa, and observed some of the strangest customs she'd ever experienced. She got caught in the multifaceted, humdrum lifestyle in the bush village of Oyubia Town, Nigeria. She saw hunger, starvation, and deprivation, as well as various diseases. She reached out with zeal and compassion to rescue, redeem, and/or relieve as many as she could, while her husband went everywhere, preaching, teaching, and administering schools. I am also indebted to her for her patience in reading this manuscript.

To Akon Johanna Otoyo, my daughter, and to Affiong (Edet Isong) Ntofon, my cousin.

They were often deprived of my presence, particularly during their formative years, when the Nigerian-Civil War raged. They gave me strength and endured my absence.

I am grateful to those who shared their insight and responded to the survey questionnaire, from which many of the facts have been documented and collated. Perhaps future generations will recognize the need to factor the problem of communication into their research. There are many areas of interest and issues to be explored; for instance, the role of elders/bishops in the church, the exercise of control within each local congregation, and the role of women—the alleged silent majority in the church.

INTRODUCTION

My scrupulous narration of the development of the Restoration Movement of the Church of Christ in Nigeria can be traced to several factors. Nigeria, the largest country in Africa, with an allegedly exploding population, has numerous religious groups. Besides a generally avowed belief in one God, they have varying doctrines and practices that have created misunderstanding and confusion among believers and unbelievers. Among the various splintered groups, curious, interested people, including skeptics, desire to know what is valid.

The motive for Martin Luther, who broke away from the Roman Catholic Church, was not to start a new church or to reform. He simply sought for the church to change the erroneous and unscriptural practices. Those who use the church for selfish, materialistic gains pose another issue. Questions have arisen whether God created the dissent in doctrines and practices.

The thrust of this book is the appointment of church leaders, the administration of the church by the high and mighty men, how offerings should be made, and the issue of the sacrament. Pluralistic Christian religion made the Restoration Movement more urgent a subject for exploration and examination.

In this book, I do not deal with ethics and morality; I deal with systems, organizational structures, the digression from biblical doctrines, and the prevalence and widespread dominance of individuals and cliques that control the general membership. Are these in consonance with scriptural doctrine? The internal struggles within the church, which often control the minds of many, have become apolitical institutions. Yet the church, if it embraces Christ's teachings, is by no means a political institution or business venture for whoever asserts to "own" it. Sections of this document also will deal with the misunderstanding of Holy Rollers, who allegedly speak in tongues and profess to heal through the instrument of the Holy Spirit.

Political agitation within the church started with the Roman Catholics, who first deviated from the scriptures, arrogating to themselves the power and right to dictate how the church should function. This action contradicts biblical teachings on the organization of the church. Elders, bishops, and presbyters, titles used synonymously, were the overseers and rulers in independent local churches, never a collection of churches to be ruled by one person or self-appointed groups of people. Later, bishops in large cities assembled to discuss common problems affecting local congregations. Decisions reached were applied to other congregations, for which they had no scriptural precedence.

The Restoration Movement argues that installing members for the oversight of the church has a biblical mandate. Competing for positions of authority would, if exercised, negate Bible teachings. For example, forbidding a class of people from marrying, eating certain foods on a given day, or tithing as an acceptable practice are not taught in the New Testament. The role of the Old Testament as precursor to the New Testament has been problematic for many. These and other such issues will be raised in this book.

> "The Spirit clearly says that in later times some will abandon the faith and follow deceiving spirits and things taught. Keep watch over yourselves and all the flock of which the Holy Spirit has made you overseers."[6]

In the understanding and practice of the restoration-movement followers, no ecclesiastical order has the prerogative to govern the church beyond what the Bible prescribed: "Be shepherds of the church of God which he bought with His own blood."[7] As a warning, Paul followed up with Acts 20:29: "I know that after I leave, savage wolves will come in among you and will not spare the flock." Paul, as protégée of Timothy and Titus, instructed them that whenever an individual desired the office of elder, he must possess the following qualifications: "The overseer must be above reproach, the husband of but one wife, temperate, hospitable, able to teach, not given to drunkenness, not violent, but gentle, not quarrelsome, not a lover of money. He must manage his own family well and see that (his children obey him) with proper respect."[8]

If a person does not marry or have a family, how would he qualify for the position of an elder, bishop, or presbyter and have an oversight of a congregation? Writing to Titus, Paul emphasized similar principles that would govern the selection of faithful individuals who sought "to govern or have the oversight of the church."[9] These scriptures are as binding today as during the first century, unless, perhaps, God has revealed, privately and independently, a new format of governance.

Inadequate human knowledge has defied God's purpose for humankind. People should not attempt to change the prescribed method of governance in the church. Several contending bishops finally capitulated, during the Council of Nicea in AD 325, for a human form of church government, whereby Augustine became the sole emperor in the West and reigned as political and religious ruler of the church. Under his reign, he relaxed Christian persecution. He ordered that confiscated church properties be returned. People, however, became suspicious of him; they doubted his sincerity or whether he fully accepted Christ, except for the purpose of using the church to achieve his materialistic, selfish gains. This was glaringly observed in his ambitious political life.[10]

The restoration movement, without being naive, felt the persuasion for change. The restorers did not advocate the dismantling of religious power structures but argued that those in religious power should step back to reexamine God's inspired approach and to teach and practice what God, through Christ, and the apostles taught.

My wide and varied experiences and my comprehension and understanding of the scriptures have equipped me with the ability to narrate the all-embracing story of the restoration movement of the Church of Christ in Nigeria, if, indeed, humankind's salvation is the focus or reason for Christian belief. Biblical remedies to bring people back to God in accordance with the scriptures are offered. I contend that evangelism should be a challenge to help elevate the physical conditions of the poor, which becomes an integral part of the movement that needs no ecclesiastical central order from which power emanates. We will observe that during the Nigerian Civil War, the restoration movement handled collaboratively the distribution of relief needs, without relying on a centralized top-down governing body. It followed the example set forth in the scriptures.

I will apply a holistic approach to averting poverty and to accepting and practicing generosity, exactly and unquestionably, in accordance with biblical teachings. Individuals should not play God, change the purpose of the scriptures or the authority of God, or substitute their will for God's.

CHAPTER 1

The Open Field

In the early seventeenth and eighteenth centuries, a small band of European merchants who sought lucrative business opportunities, particularly in human trade, had a great impact on the African continent. Upon reaching the coastal regions, they cajoled, enticed, and, in some cases, bludgeoned Africans into passivity, using the threat of guns. Missionaries who also came in the seventeenth century were faced with the politics of establishing mission posts. The chiefs desired education and hospitals. The chiefs and middlemen who capitulated to the ambitions of the white man became the source from which freed men and women, some already in servitude to the local chiefs, were captured and bargained for Missionaries that were often, in collusion with the merchants.

The missionaries encountered people whose religions were animistic, believing that spirits inhabited nonliving objects. These spirits, they assumed, possessed immense power with a self-consciousness that could be manipulated to control the habits and behavior of humans. The spirits influenced human lives, but they also inhabited observable objects, like the whole realm of the raging ocean, the cosmic stars in their brilliance, the towering, majestic mountains and hills, the crocodile, the anthills, trees, and all in their magnificence. These reflected, for them, the existence and manifestations of powerful beings or gods. Each tribe attributed divinity to a god that fulfilled their individual physical and psychological needs, a god that could preserve, prolong, or destroy their lives. Each god had special powers that controlled the physical and metaphysical realm beyond human consciousness and could be approached differently for perceived favors.

The agents of the new religion, Christian missionaries, had to combat and supplant the pantheistic religious beliefs and practices of the natives, to whom Christianity was alien because it had no visible object with which they could identify.

Old habits, especially entrenched values and beliefs, do not perish easily. Some do so by force, giving way to new ideas. Others, in time and depending on the perceived benefits or new values, give way to behaviors, ethos that provide a better way of life for the practitioners. In Nigeria, as in other communities, people generally cling tenaciously to their denominational views and practices, rather than the possibility of adopting teachings and religious practices that are alien. Christianity, with its monolithic view, has been viewed by many as a white man's religion. Change never gives way easily to new forms of behavior; it was lingering around the corner.

Though many uphold the Bible as God's inspired written words, its teachings, dogmas, and injunctions, which should elicit compliance and serve as a medium of unification, have caused a splintering into aberrant, contesting groups with varied interpretations of the scriptures. Every denomination has its special hierarchy of control where it originated, with special laws, rules, and policies that are generated from the top echelon to control the spiritual life and demand conformity from the communicants. The concept of ecumenism, which has been touted for years, appears to be a farce because churches have deviated from the system of governance required in the New Testament.

God's immutable, inveterate words were revealed through prophets and the apostles, through dreams, visions, or direct illumination, of which God's servants had to accept and speak as authoritative divine injunctions. There has been a clear denial of God's commands for not teaching and practicing the same things scripturally.

Since we are many and different, it is impossible to think alike or to act similarly. The argument for many is that every individual, church, or denomination that calls on God's name is heard, regardless of how we approach him, whether or not we strive to be united, speak the same thing, or abide by the same scriptural principles. This thinking has given rise to the fallacy of justifying our ignorance—to speak where the Bible speaks and to be silent where the Bible is silent.

> And the Spirit and the bride say, "Come And let him who hears say, "Come" And let him who is thirsty come and, whoever will, let him take the water of life freely For I testify to everyone who hears the words of the prophecy of this book, if anyone adds to him the plagues that are written in this book. If anyone will take away from the words of the book of this prophesy, God will take away his part out of the tree of life, and out of the holy city, and the things that are written this book."[11]

Three years after the end of the Second World War, Nigeria was poised to embrace a new political arena of social and religious change. Very few people could have predicted the nature, scope, and direction of the change about to erupt. Many Nigerian veterans who returned home from the war had experienced and assimilated diverse cultural values through their interaction with other soldiers in various sectors of military engagement. These men and women began to see their country, which was vested with the accoutrements of colonial imperialism, in a different perspective.

Colonial power interest in Nigeria was total dominance, pillaging, and draining the country's meager resources. These veterans had witnessed other cultures in action and clamored for similar treatment of equality and self-expression. At this stage, Coolidge Okon Akpan (C. A. O.) Essien already was immersed in denominational doctrine, due to his discontent with the prevailing dysfunctional churches. He saw an open door to share the concept and teachings of the New Testament church with as many people as he could.

The Carrot-and-Stick Conversions

The early denominations—Methodist, Roman Catholic, Episcopalian, and Baptist—that already had established schools were producing catechists, teachers, and, in some instances, court clerks. Initially, these groups admitted mostly children of communicants of the respective religious denominations into their schools. Parents who became aware of the materialistic, external intrinsic, and economic value of Western formal education succumbed to the lure and unwritten code of conversion as a prerequisite for admission into the schools. Religious doctrine was not generally propagated or open to honest discussion and decision-making. Members were not literate so they could not read, understand, or interpret the scriptures. Some churches never allowed the members to own or read the Bible. Consequently, the priest or the ministers who made the initial contact with village heads interpreted the Bible in their own ways, depending on their individual church dogma.

Enrollment in schools and/or participation for medical care were granted only to communicants, whose parents consented for candidacy in the mission church. Conversion was based on the proverbial carrot-and-stick principle. These parents had no other choice but to succumb to the pressure to educate their children in the mission schools. The avowed intentions of a few religious denominations were not to use schools or any social service as bait to attract converts. Instead, they, like John the Baptist, stood on street corners and in marketplaces, proclaiming their respective brands of the gospel.

The Era of Political Struggle

The Second World War was an avenger of horrible, destructive events in the lives of families and the nation. It also helped to spearhead a sense of discovery and a chance to question traditional views, values, and practices, whether in government, religion, or social or political arenas. Individuals and local communicants felt the need to participate in activities directed at determining their destinies. According to John B. Grimley and Gordon F. Robinson, the Second World War brought an awakening to Nigeria that began with the youth. The army took young men to faraway places. They fought side by side with British soldiers, and some received commissions. Many who had no education enlisted in schools, where they acquired training in trades and services that was valuable to the army and potentially valuable in civilian life. They visited foreign countries and assimilated with different people whose ideas, though strange, influenced them.[12]

Though Nigeria remained largely illiterate, the small number who could read and write were concentrated in large cities, like Lagos, Calabar, Enugu, Ibadan, Kaduna, and Port Harcourt. They found sanctuaries in villages as teachers and police officers and in the court systems. They were curious, excited, avid readers, who sought avenues for self-enlightenment and improvement. By the end of the Second World War, when those who had been stationed abroad returned to their villages, they had been torn from ingrained ancestral ways. This period was the dawning of a new age that sparked new and determined aspirations for education. Those who had dropped out of school enrolled in correspondence courses, the completion of which would lead them to earn the coveted diplomas that enabled them to gain employment. A host of others sought religion, not for spirituality but as avenues for materialistic self-improvement.

Nigerian veterans became the banner-bearers. They assimilated new values, and they began to see their society with keen eyes and a sense of nationalism. The political arena in Nigeria was on edge. Several religious bodies descended on the country, teaching their curious brands of religion. Agitation for independence by a nucleus of Nigerians, like H. S. Macauley, a descendant of Bishop Samuel Crowther, and many of his protégés who had been educated abroad, began clamoring for freedom for Nigeria from the restrictive claws of colonial imperialism. Within a few short years, they sought to wrest political power from the colonial masters who ruled the country. Men like the late Dr. Nnamdi Azikiwe, Obafeme Awolowo, and Professor Eyo Ita joined Herbert Macaulay to rouse public opinion against British governance. On the other hand, the religious atmosphere was superficially calm, while each denomination competed, using the establishment of schools and hospitals as drawing cards to proselytes.

CHAPTER 2

The Plea for Reason and Ecumenism

The Church of Christ started in Nigeria in 1948. Two years after its advent and among well-established groups, its message aroused skepticism and mixed acceptance. Even with the expansion of Nigeria's growing population, the church was yet to emerge as a welcome factor. Those who came to hear the exposition of fallacies in denominational doctrines and practices became agitated, if not provoked.

In some communities, when the Church of Christ established its first Bible school in 1954, the members were viewed as rabble-rousers. Many denominational members and their priests hardly studied the Bible contextually or its systemic format. They spoke in generalities, without reference to specific scriptures, in defense of their positions; if they did use specifics, they were twisted, and contextual elaboration was absent. Many depended exclusively on the priest and their "reverend fathers" to read, translate, and/or interpret the scriptures.

For example, the Catholics have consistently taught the doctrine of the seven sacraments: (1) baptism, which is to pour water three times on the recipient's head; (2) confirmation, a religious act that confirms and strengthens baptism of grace to the convert; (3) the Eucharist, also called the Blessed Sacrament, for which the individual participates in the observation of the symbolic transformation of bread and wine to the real body and blood of Jesus, called *transubstantiation*; (4) penance or reconciliation—forgiveness after confession; (5) anointing of the sick; (6) holy orders; and (7) marriage.

Members, therefore, swallowed whatever the priest dished out without question—hook, line, and sinker. There was a time when members of the Roman Catholic Church were prohibited from opening the Bible, thereby restricting any inquisitive desire to study it. This position resulted in what was known as the "chain Bible," with its origin in Italy. Many errors still persist.

Church of Christ preachers who came on the scene began advocating for a return to the New Testament path. They beckoned the general religious public to "stop doing wrong, learn to do right, seek justice, encourage the oppressed, defend the cause of the fatherless, plead the cause of the widows. Come now, says the Lord, let us reason together"[13]

Paul the apostle wrote, urging people to study the scriptures, saying that a systematic study, rather than escalate the continuing schisms in Christendom, would unfold how humanity could unite, based on the teachings of the Son of God and the apostles.

Religious underpinnings, instead of uniting humankind, perpetuates the dividing of people into small, atomistic units of believers. The scheme of redemption from God to humans will make humans approved by God, furnish humans for every good work, and free humans from the pernicious doctrines of humankind.

The advocacy of the denominations has been a movement that envisions collectivism that binds people to an ecclesiastical central authority, where task performance emanates from the top. Martin Luther saw the havoc of hierarchical arrangement that bound people to that central authority, which expatiated countless unholy practices. The system that bound people to a central authority naturally kept people ignorant of God's Word.

The era of discontentment in Nigeria made it a hot bed for religious activism and intolerance. This was a period that fractionalized the people a lot more than tribal cleavages and into more splintered religious groups. The scores of creed books and catechisms, originating from various established churches, were designed to force their members to ignore the Bible as the authoritative will of God, which gauged governance in the church. Denominations devised practices of governance that were contained in their "books of faith," not the Bible as the ultimate reference book. As academically and intellectually astute as many have been, their minds were seared, according to Paul. The Spirit clearly says "that in later times, some will abandon the faith and follow deceiving spirits and things taught by demons. Such teachings come through hypocritical liars, whose consciences have been seared as with a hot iron, so that they believe a lie."[14]

It is easy to continue to uphold a value or practice without understanding whether the foundation of the belief was biblically justified. Taking a critical look and assiduously examining the tenets of a particular belief or doctrine is encouraged in the scriptures; for instance, Jesus exhorted the scribes and Pharisees,

> "For the very work that the father has given me to finish, and which I am doing, testify that the Father has sent me. And the Father who sent me has himself testified concerning me. You have never heard his voice, nor seen his form, nor does his words dwell in you, for you do not belief the one he sent. You diligently study the Scriptures because you think that by them you possess eternal life. These are the Scriptures that testify about me."[15]

Again, in agreement with Christ's words, Paul stated that the Bereans examined and searched the scriptures daily to determine the veracity of his teaching. On arriving there [Berea], they went to the Jewish synagogue.

"Now the Bereans were of more noble character than the Thessalonians, for they received the message with great eagerness and examined the scriptures every day to see if what Paul said was true."[16]

Many people have been unwilling to search the scriptures or have simply surrendered to their priests or bishops, who perhaps knew extraordinarily little or knew the implication of a passage but would not countenance it as a guide.

Church of Christ proponents who set in motion the restoration movement knew, besides the obvious prevailing religious intolerance, that the reformation movement was flawed. The Bible, not human creeds, was the only rule of faith from 1950 to about 1960. Few people in Nigeria knew of the restoration movement, and if they knew, they failed to recognize the implications of it. They were content with the prevailing religious conditions and attitudes and felt at ease; they were not ready or willing to accommodate new ideas. Many were, like the Jews, ignorant of God's righteousness, and being so ignorant, they proceeded to arrogate to themselves their own righteousness."[17]

With the advent of the church in some areas, new ideas initially were nonthreatening to the general religious public. Gradually, as large groups of already-established churches flocked to the will of Christ, those who stood akimbo soon realized the threat posed by the church.

In many communities, the church thrived and began to sprout roots. Some denominational groups banded together to foil the movement because it raised its voice to challenge and expose false teachings and practices.

Cao Essien: One Man Can Make A Difference

Figure 1

Human history is replete with individuals who, either through divine guidance or self-motivation, stepped up to engineer social, political, or religious change. What these self-appointed individuals chose to do, in many ways, reshaped the direction of their lives, community, and/or nation. The changes they aspired to enact often were met with opposition or danger and were painful. They were misunderstood or dubbed as upstarts and rebellious radicals. These people did not fully understand the direction or the impact of their missions on the lives of those who would be affected.

God's Providence

> God moves in a Mysterious Way
> His wonders to perform.
> He plans His footsteps in the sea.
> And rides upon the storm.[18]

The following section is the story of Coolidge Okon Akpan (C. A. O.) Essien. Through his own initiative and willingness, he searched for, accepted, and followed the divine plan of redemption. He diligently sought God's knowledge, first for his salvation and then to educate people to a better knowledge of God's divine will. In his pursuit, he changed the fractured religious and social landscape. His message touched many lives and reached not only his immediate village community but thousands and millions of lives in distant parts of Africa.

Dramatic stories are not always staged; they find their places in the hearts and lives of men and women who accept the values and inspiration expounded through the Messiah. But Essien was not a messiah. He was a simple, approachable, ordinary man. He was not a prodigy by any standard, nor was he from the aristocracy. He was an agrarian, but he had no mass acreage of land by which he could generate enough assets and income to support his ambition for a spiritually dying people. God's providential inspiration guided him, one might say, in a mysterious way, through skepticism, discouragement, and opposition.

People have given accounts of their knowledge of C. A. O. Essien, and there is a thread of commonality in the narrations. The following accounts are from individuals whose descriptions are untainted and unprejudiced. They knew him. They worked with him and can bear witness to his life and work. People like V. V. Akpan, George Fearless Akpan, Essien Ekanem, and James Eton, who preached at the early stages of the restoration movement to Igbos, attested to his pedigree and pecuniary status.

Etim Asuquo, a veteran minister of the Lawanson Church of Christ at Surulere, Lagos, wrote, "Essien was an officer in the Nigerian Police Force. George U. Ekong one of the first converts and Essien's protégée, attested to Essien as having been an X-Police officer, a tall and huge black man with a smiling countenance." He was "kind, sympathetic, approachable, and patient with people." He further described Essien as one who knew about human relations, which became an asset and contributed to his success in winning souls for Christ.[19] These personal attributes endeared him to the people, a characteristic that transcended tribal and ethnic differences in a multilinguistic nation like Nigeria.

Effiong Okon Essien, the brother of C. A. O. Essien, in response to a questionnaire, wrote, "Most of the things that I have said are eyewitness accounts, while others are derived from records that have been left behind by C. A. O. Essien himself, and from Brothers Essien Ekanem, J. U. Akpan, Effiong Atte Enyenihi, and J. R. Eton," who corroborated the authenticity of the narration. According to his brother, C. A. O. Essien's birth was heralded, as with most children, as a blessing. "A baby was born to Okon Essien Ukpong and Adiaha Inyang Antia on April 15, 1915, at the little village of Ikot Usen, Ibiono near Itu, formerly Southeastern Region of Nigeria and now Akwa Ibom State."[20]

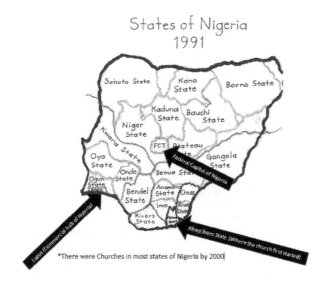

Figure 2

Map of Nigeria

Figure 3

Howard and Mildred Horton,
First American Missionary

In Effiong Okon Essien's unpublished *History of the Church*, he wrote,

> "This was Coolidge Asuquo Okon Essien, the earthen vessel who was destined to be God's instrument for carrying the gospel of Christ, as other young people of his day, young Asuquo was exposed to Western education as taught by the Presbyterian Church. Essien completed his formal education and became an apprentice carpenter at the Hope Waddell Training Institute, Calabar, and later joined the Nigerian Police force 1938–1940."[21]

His career as a police officer was short-lived. He became disenchanted over the moral and ethical decadence of his fellow officers; "some, he felt, were criminals" His dissatisfaction continued to escalate, and finally, he gave up his job and returned to his village, where he spent his time in contemplation, personal reading of the Bible, and correspondence courses, in which he enrolled from various tuition houses in Europe and America. From his personal studies, he came to understand that the name and doctrines of the church which he was a member were unscriptural. So, he resigned his membership from the Presbyterian Church and joined the Pentecostal Assemblies of the World. He was baptized and ordained as a pastor of that denomination."[22] As events unfolded, this change was, again, short-lived.

Prior to the advent of the Church of Christ in Nigeria, the Church of Scotland Mission had established schools and churches among the Efik-speaking people. Famous among the missionaries was the undaunted young missionary Mary Slessor, whose immense spirit of love and human compassion won the hearts of many. She was instrumental in saving the lives of twins abandoned to die, resulting from superstition that twins were harbingers of evil in the family. Mary Slessor and C. A. O. Essien were contemporaries, serving people at different parts of the same region.

CHAPTER 3

Hands across the Ocean

Lawrence Avenue Church of Christ
(Essien's Search for Affiliation)

During the period of 1944–1948, events developed in the United States that were destined to affect the establishment of the church in Nigeria. As Reda C. Goff wrote in *The Great Nigerian Mission*,

> "The story started eight years prior to the realization of Essien's dream It started on May 2, 1944 when the Lawrence Avenue Church (now Concord Road Church of Christ) met for their regular monthly meeting. None of those who met were aware of the historical implications and significance of that meeting. Rhetorically, who could have even dreamed that the salvation of thousands, perhaps the entire nation, might hinge on the decision of their small gathering."[23]

Three weeks later, the report of the committee—already set up to determine the possibility and the logistics for establishing a Bible correspondence course designed to serve American servicemen—was presented. The business meeting was called to order by Brother John Shacklet at 8:00 p.m., with a prayer by Brother W. H. Bennett. The Bible correspondence course was adopted with a monthly budget of seven hundred to one thousand dollars. Other pertinent issues connected with the initiation and involvement of the Bible correspondence course were discussed. The motion by Brother Shacklet for the acceptance of the correspondence course was approved and adopted. "This was the great decision made; one that would affect thousands of people."[24]

While it was the desire and intent of Lawrence Avenue Church of Christ to initiate a Bible correspondence course for US servicemen overseas, it was reasoned that the course would also impact the spiritual lives of many in Africa. There were speculations as to how C. A. O. Essien had come in contact with Ms. Anna-Maria Braum. One common view is that he must have picked up religious materials on the street, one of which contained the address of Ms. Braum, offering the correspondence course, or that someone informed him of a radio broadcast from South Africa. To buttress this view, the proponents offered the fact that Nigerians were avid readers who thirsted to improve their educational level and lifestyle;

they scavenged for whatever reading materials they could glean. Others suggested that a Peace Corps worker must have accidentally dropped a postcard, which a passer-by picked up. That postcard contained derogatory but true information about Nigerians' habit of unabashedly relieving themselves on the street. This incident raised an uproar, causing an international and political wedge between Nigeria and the United States. Someone must have picked up a note that indicated Ms. Maria Braum was soliciting English teachers or teachers for Bible correspondence course.

During the Second World War, however, Nigerian enlistees fought side by side with British soldiers, which ended three years prior to C. A. O. Essien emerging as a dominant force in the establishment of the Church of Christ in Nigeria. During the war, servicemen had interacted with people of different cultures, sharing magazines and newspapers of various kinds. They had listened to world radio broadcasting news and religious programs that originated from the United States, Europe, and South Africa.

A more plausible and historically documented view is that C. A. O. Essien must have gotten Ms. Braum's address from a friend who had access to a serviceman. George U. Ekong stated, "Essien, already a Pentecostal member, was religiously inclined [and] either paid for or received the advertised address of a free Bible correspondence course from a friend who perhaps was reading magazines and religious materials that readily fell into the hands of a Nigerians friend."

During this period, historically, Nigerians ordered shoes, holy water, prayer handkerchiefs, and paraphernalia from quack religious groups of all sorts, from addresses found on the streets or from friends who were already in contact with individuals and churches abroad—America being the major export area. Essien already had received Bible correspondence courses from many sources, but none of these had exposed him to what he was yet to learn. He was, perhaps, a dreamer, nurturing the hope of establishing contact with other Bible correspondence groups, hopeful that he would discover that which appealed to him. Fortunately, upon patient research and numerous correspondences, he contacted Ms. Maria Braum with the following message and address:

> "Miss A. M. Braum, 13b Mundchen 15, Lindwurmstrassee 126a, Germany (Bavaria) US Zone: With great pleasure I received your lessons today. My time is limited, and I cannot promise to attend them. But I shall not hesitate to read them over when I have the leisure at my disposal, for I am working long hours each day. But I think the idea wonderful

and shall do the best to interest as many Germans as possible in your scheme and I trust you will provide me with the good text."[25]

Anna Maria Braum would become the vital link in the chain of the destiny of the Nigerian church planting during the following years. It was never known whether Ms. Braum was a member of the body of Christ or not, the purpose for Miss Braum establishing the "Internationals Korresponenz-Buro in Munich, Germany, after the war in 1945, was to promote the learning of languages, English in particular through the practice of letter writing between pen-pals among the Germans."[26] C. A. O. Essien enrolled in the Bible correspondence course in July 1948, and the unusual return address Ibiaku, Ikot Usen, Ibiono, Itu, Nigeria, West Africa attracted instant notice. He was introduced to Lawrence Avenue Church of Christ by Miss. Braum, from whom he had requested a good recommendation of a Bible correspondence program. Essien's enrollment and grade card number 4665 for the first twenty-four lessons were all perfect. While studying the lessons, he unselfishly shared his newfound knowledge of the scriptures with others. without hesitation, he contacted and taught his people.

We cannot underestimate the psychological impact of a foreign European or American presence in the scope and nature of the program. Many saw the Americans as great conquistadors and liberators or flag bearers, who had just emerged victorious from the Second World War. Essien reached out to invite them to visit Nigeria.

Figure 4

First Church of Christ Building at Ikot Usen, Ibiono

Expatriates Enter the Scene
(A Dream Come True)

Essien recruited and trained a cadre of young men who would ultimately become itinerant evangelist messengers, beginning in 1948, going into every nook and cranny to deliver the unadulterated gospel. He also had fifty congregations of the apostolic Church of Christ that were introduced to the same Bible correspondence course. Meanwhile, with such an astounding report of conversions, Lawrence Avenue Church of Christ desired to authenticate and assess the validity of the claim and enormity of the work.

Lawrence Avenue Church of Christ contacted Brother Brown, who was sponsored by Central Church of Christ in Nashville, Tennessee, in South Africa. Meanwhile, Essien continued appealing for tracts, Bibles, and study materials. He also urged them to send missionary helpers. Lawrence Avenue, as a small congregation that didn't know the magnitude of such an undertaking and involvement, felt reticent, initially, to commit to sending missionaries. Essien, though perturbed, was persistent in his appeal for missionaries. He remembered Christ's statement on persistence: "Seek and ye shall find, knock for it shall be opened unto you."[27] The presence of foreign missionaries would lend credibility, as their experience would be an asset of immeasurable proportions to the work.

Finally, Lawrence Avenue Church of Christ took the first step. Although still skeptical, they felt that by sending Bibles, tracts, commentaries, and Communion cups, they would not lose anything. Later, they decided to send Boyd Rees and Eldred Echols of Nowhe Mission Southern Rhodesia, South Africa, to investigate the claims and the scope of the work. The report of Rees and Echols was a classic comprehensive work that was reprinted and circulated throughout the brotherhood of the Churches of Christ in the United States. They reported of the mass conversion of 340 in a day during the visit.

After the report was made public, it took a period of absorption and evaluation before Lawrence Avenue Church made a firm decision. After much deliberation, Lawrence Avenue decided to launch into the dark terrain of the West Coast of Africa. G. Ekong further narrated that some of the trained itinerant preachers were working tirelessly with C. A. O. Essien, teaching the young congregations. There were men like V. V. Akpan, George Ekong, Fearless Akpan, Essien Ekanem, and Effiong Atte Enyenihi in Efik Ibibio province, as well as Brother James Ezineo, who were diligently working among new churches. The list of the initial thriving churches prior to the arrival of the resident missionaries in 1952 is as follows:

Ikot Usen, 80 members	Ntan Ekere, 140 members
Ikot Ebom, 60 members	Ibiaku Ikot Oku, 96 members
Usuk Ibiaku Uruan, 180 members	Okobo Ibiono, 80 members
Ikpedip, 60 members	Ikot Mbuk, 65 members
Obio Ibiono, 80 members	Ikot Mbuk, 65 members[28]

The above churches became the springboard from which numerous churches followed. The members from these new churches had a limited understanding of the teachings of the New Testament church, other than rudimentary doctrinal issues. The need for long-term missionaries was acute. Knowing the importance of sound teaching for the new, young, immature preachers, Essien was persistent in his appeal for Lawrence Avenue Church of Christ to send missionaries, as the indigent ministers' level of understanding of the scriptures was inadequate to meet the challenges they would encounter. "We can teach our people, but we need teaching ourselves Send people to teach us and we shall take Nigeria for Christ."[29] Ambitious, bold, and visionary, he was right. Later, Lawrence Avenue leaders capitulated. Then followed the arrival of long-term resident missionary families, of which Jimmy Johnson was the first to arrive on November 2, 1952, while Howard Horton arrived on November 7, 1952.

A cadre of preachers, taught by Essien in two weeks, later expanded to three-month short-term Bible courses. These preachers were P. A. Alfred, D. E. Akpan, J. H. Akpan, E. S. Ntuk, H. E. Ene, Bassey Utuk, J. I. Chuku, A. W. Akpan, Effiong Atte Enyenihi, G. M. Ntuk, J. R. Eton, A. K. Onwusoro, D. D. Isonguyo, N. R. Umana, and E. Ekanem; many other young Christians also were trained. These men formed the nucleus of a zealous group of dedicated men who "went everywhere preaching and establishing churches. Most of these men were used, according to Etim Asuquo, "as teachers, preachers, and interpreters."[30] They led the missionaries to places they never had anticipated, returning home late at night, exhausted.

There was stark realization of the need for intensive long-term training Short-term Bible courses, though helpful, provided a temporary first-aid fix, furnishing the preachers with some rudimentary information to enable them to meet the spiritual challenges of the growing congregations. Brother Effiong O. Essien wrote,

> "The addition of Eugene Peden, in October 1956, and Elvis Huffard in December 14, 1955 was significant. These men made an excellent team. Etim Asuquo's narrative gave additional names of missionaries who arrived later

and these being, Wendell Broom, Burney
E. Bawcom, Billy Nicks, and Tommy
Kelton."[31]

Tommy Kelton was daring and unencumbered by
red tape. In an unusual fashion, he cleared his personal
luggage from customs without assistance, loaded his
luggage in a van, and drove the more than four hundred
rough and treacherous miles from Lagos to Ikot Usen,
a feat no missionary had ever done. At the time, all the
missionaries lived at Ikot Usen, and later, some of them
moved to Ukpom, Abak.

The three-month Bible training course that Brother
C. A. O. Essien initiated in 1948 was only a head-start
program, designed to maintain the faith of the young
and inexperienced new converts. They needed pertinent
scriptural information, a theological and hermeneutical
knowledge of the scriptures so they could articulate
intelligently the essential elements of the scheme of
redemption. This would enhance a better understanding
of the scriptures, offering the students something to
which they could hang on. While many were unschooled
in basic schematic information, they asserted themselves
and ventured into the open fields. Essien formalized his
outline of the Bible correspondence course into lesson
plans, which he used to train the neophytes. The three-
month program was short-term but advantageous to the

churches that adopted the process for individual church development until the arrival of the missionaries.

Effective service to the local churches was always paramount in the minds of the missionaries. Knowing that church leaders, including evangelists, had not adequate or sound Bible knowledge to maintain the churches, training preachers and leaders became of urgent importance. Moral principles, love, kindness, mercy, and forgiveness, as enunciated by the teachings of Christ, were major components of the curriculum. Other areas of concern were doctrinal issues, such as the establishment of the New Testament church, the synoptic gospels, denominational doctrines, candidates for baptism, faith and grace, methods of raising funds for the church, the structure and governance of the church, and other related issues. These were also short fixes.

In September 1953, twelve men were selected for additional intensive training, as stated in Howard Horton's report. They received intensive studies in the New Testament church, church history, religious errors, church problems, preparation and delivery of sermons, hermeneutics, and apologetics. The arrival of Eugene Paden and his family on October 12, 1955, reduced the burden shouldered by two missionaries. His zestful and deep sense of commitment endeared him to many Nigerians. The intensity of his efforts was instrumental in the conversion of many souls and the establishment of many churches. Glen Martin's reaction to Eugene Peden was,

> "Peden has done an excellent job of constructing the buildings, keeping the books, and stabilizing the work. It is hard to realize that one man could have done so much. To my mind, he is deserving of special commendation from the congregation of Lawrence Avenue Church of Christ."[32]

As churches were established, membership increased. There were church leaders, ministers, and members whose voices were not of dissatisfaction with what the missionaries were doing but of genuine concern over the advancement of biblical knowledge. The short-term course was inadequate. Preachers needed advanced and broad-based, solid, long-term biblical training. Howard Horton's report reflected the sentiments voiced by many, stating,

> "Since our first short courses last year (1953) Brother Johnson and I have been fully aware that three months cannot suffice to prepare men to preach the gospel. We have pondered the matter and often prayed. At least two years will

> be required to prepare men with even a
> minimum knowledge of the truth and
> to develop their abilities to distinguish
> common popular denominational
> errors."[33]

In 2002, after forty-two years of independence, the Canadian prime minister Jean Chretien observed that Africa had long suffered from poverty, racial discrimination, tribal warfare, diseases, and inadequate preparation for positions of leadership. Many members required secular and biblical training conjointly to educate the next generation of Christians.

If this observation was made in 2002, what chances were there for the Nigerian churches in 1953 to 2002, most of which had emerged from agrarian communities, to cooperatively produce the financial resources needed for stabilizing the faith of weak Christians? How could they, under such unfavorable conditions, instill sound conceptual knowledge of the scriptures? Or how could they, without external resources, establish, independently, the type of institution they advocated?

Because of the economic conditions in the country, members were strapped, without the material resources to venture into the establishment of a religious institution that they sought. To truly develop an indigenously sponsored school or actively functional church, they needed an investment of large sums of money that the churches, at that stage, did not possess.

The church, by doctrine, has not been a central ecclesiastical system that generates and doles out funds to the local churches. They must demonstrate their ability to provide the resources and the material necessity to sustain envisioned projects. There must be a collaborative, shared decision-making process among those involved for a project to be truly native, without external financing. The tribal and geopolitical environment and the concept of individual church autonomy, for which there was mounting opposition, became impediments. These adverse conditions, especially lack of money, made the notion of the churches' involvement in establishing secular institutions, supported through local church funds, impossible. Besides the inherent ideological doctrinal issues, no single church, or a combination of churches in the 1940s and 1960s could undertake such a project—at least not yet.

The Christian Schools

Leaders of churches—least realizing their yearnings, including agitations by some activist members—had made some impact in the hearts of the missionaries, especially Howard Horton. The missionaries quietly contemplated what course of action to take to acquiesce to the wishes of the people. To explore the prospect of an expanded educational program in the country, according to Reda Goff, "Horton flew to Nashville, Tennessee on August 11, 1953 for a two-week conference with the Elders of Lawrence Avenue Church of Christ."[34]

Howard Horton, in his report to Lawrence Avenue Church and supporting churches, wrote, "We are also quite confident that there is an expanding nucleus of 'gold, silver, and precious stones', which will stand inspite of fiery trials. The rapid growth created problems, but with the problems came unlimited opportunities to teach and to save some."[35]

It was assumed, among other issues, that during the very inchoate stages of the church development, Horton envisaged the stabilizing effect and the role schools played in nurturing strong Christian beliefs and principles. Included were the need for personnel and resources. The added managerial duties would detract from their foremost mandate and objectives. Also, supporting congregations, at the time, had no budget to invest in the administration of schools. As they debated the merits of taking over the supervision of schools, many communities wished to relinquish responsibility to the church. At some point, sound judgment prevailed, forcing the missionaries to cave into the pleas of the members.

The advantages of administering schools as a peripheral means of preaching and proselytizing and for engaging young minds toward acquisition of biblical knowledge was unarguably overwhelming. Parents who left leading denominational schools and churches desired that their children be provided vibrant religious instruction. Howard Horton, conscious of the dilemma and the intrinsic value of Christian education as a means of infusing biblical principles, enlightenment, and for strengthening the faith of young churches, was ahead of the times in thought and vision. He needed expatriate workers who had the discipline, ability, training, and experience to administer the schools handed over to the Church of Christ.

On November 4, 1953, Elvis Huffard, his wife, Emily, and their three children arrived in Nigeria. Howard Horton, Jimmy Johnson, and Gene Peden, who were already in Nigeria, were available to assist Huffard, whose arrival ushered in a new direction of missionary activities, which was in response to the yearnings of the people.

A progressive, dynamic movement cannot survive with crude and untested tools to implement change. They needed tested and fundamentally sound personnel. From the outset, Huffard felt that the greatest needs and challenges of churches were lack of biblical knowledge and practical application by and for every baptized believer. Elvis Huffard's shoes were big enough to handle the duties and responsibilities of the Christian elementary schools. After surveying and determining the needs of the existing schools, he soon set-in motion a systematic approach to managing the ten schools that were handed to the mission.

Ukpom Bible Training School became a beacon of light in a tempestuous sea of darkness. It was also a place for men in search of the truth, which essentially was the only weapon to engage in spiritual warfare.

In all phases of its studies, it provided the weapon to combat and expose religious errors and brought hope through God's grace and the redemption that his Son, Jesus, offers freely to all believers. Those who graduated showed astuteness as they went among villages and towns, proclaiming the unadulterated good news of the redemptive power of Jesus Christ.

Someone said that he who would truly fight for injustice must do so as a private man, not in public, if he means to preserve his life, even for a short time. The graduates at Ukpom were aware of the dangers, the ridicule, and the abuse in a hostile environment. But they were undaunted, prevailing as they went about teaching and preaching. Ukpom Bible Training School's first graduates provided the stimulus that the movement needed to move in different directions.

The Christian (Elementary) Schools

Don Harrison, our beloved "workhorse," accompanied by his wife, Joyce, served as a missionary, teacher, and an administrator at the Christian Secondary Technical College. Elvis Huffard saw a new trend of work—the added responsibility of administrating ten elementary Christian schools, which were handed over by various communities to the Nigerian Mission (now African Christian Schools) management. Ukpom Bible School teachers were recruited to primarily teach the Bible in the elementary schools. Other communities without Churches of Christ allowed their community schools to be managed by the church, and from that, many other churches were established.

Six years had elapsed since the emergence of the church in Nigeria. Churches were spreading in different directions like wildfire. Ukpom Bible School graduates waited in the wings eagerly, ready to make the bold adventure into many corners of Nigeria.

At this stage, the church was young, and missionaries initially were not accustomed to the need to embark on the establishment and management of educational institutions, as already pioneered by the denominations. Requests (or demands) by church adherents for the missionaries to become involved in the establishment of secular institutions were rebuffed initially. The resistance was understandably temporary, as the missionaries argued that their major and primary objective was to preach and teach the gospel, without engaging in the establishment of secular institutions. Adherents argued that their children would be forced to attend and participate in denominational doctrines and practices. They said they could not send their children to denominational schools and expect them to become faithful, nor should they make sacrifices that were spiritually detrimental to their children's spiritual growth.

The missionaries insisted that they were sent to evangelize; pursuing other objectives would distract from their primary aims. Also, the churches that sponsored them operated on minimal budgets that excluded involvement in the management of schools. As the church grew, some of the missionaries saw the need, and as they debated the merits of accepting the arduous task of administering schools, they were torn between their original goals and the community's strong appeal for them to accept the challenge to establish and manage secular institutions.

Shortly, the positive effect of running schools, whereby young men and women acquire firm biblical knowledge, became evident. Parents who left the leading denominational schools desired that their children be provided instruction that would enable them to avoid the demonic false teachings. Howard Horton became the man to articulate to American churches the importance and benefits of a Christian institution that would enlighten and stabilize the faith of members. Howard had moved a step ahead and already was deeply involved in the search for a person with the educational administrative ability, training, and experience for the task of administering schools. At this stage, Howard P. Horton began to influence the expansion of the Nigerian evangelistic mission work.

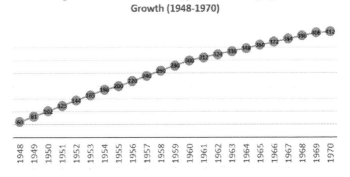

Nigerian Churches of Christ Approximated Congregation Growth (1948-1970)

Figure 5

Horton had his advanced degrees from Pepperdine and David Lipscomb Colleges. He was encouraged by Eldred Echols regarding the opportunity of evangelistic work in Nigeria. He said he had prayed to God for wisdom and effectiveness as he contemplated entering Nigeria; without God's guidance and blessing, their hopes and dreams would falter. Upon arriving in Nigeria in 1952, he met the following pillars of the movement: C. A. O. Essien, P. A. Alfred, Fearless Akpan, P. U. Akpan, E. A. Ekanem, and, later, Effiong Atte Enyenihi, men with whom he worked closely.

Upon arrival, he wrote that they lived in the thatched

mud building constructed by Ikot Usen village on the church compound. "Ikot Usen village was very hospitable when we arrived late at night. Many villagers helped to unload enough bedding for us to sleep for the first few days." The village had scheduled a very elaborate reception for them. "Everything was new to us and we were new to the people. Everyone was especially interested in our children, Ann and Angela, who perhaps were the first American children they ever saw." Since no American had preceded them in this village, they relied heavily on the counsel of Brother Essien. When asked about orientation, Horton wrote, "In the first three weeks, he [Essien] and I visited all the sixty-four congregations of the Churches of Christ, and this was a great orientation for me."[36]

His primary work was in the then-Southeastern Region in the Cross River (currently Akwa Ibom State), excluding the time at Ogoja, which, under the present geopolitical arrangement, has been merged with Calabar as Cross River. "However, I made many trips into Igboland, across the Cross River-eastward, and one exploratory mission west of the Nigeria River, that has become the Delta State."[37]

In the last four months, there were three thousand baptisms and twenty new congregations. Horton reported to the *Christian Chronicle* (a major Church of Christ–affiliated publishing company) that there were about a hundred baptisms per month by Nigerian and Americans together: "In my newsletter of October 31, 1957, I reported that baptisms were averaging one hundred to three hundred per month. I personally helped in baptisms when, on one day, groups of fifties, forties, and thirties would present themselves in obedience to Christ." To encourage these new converts, most of whom never had a Bible, he wrote, "We made it a practice to present each new church with an Efik Bible [and] a bottle of communion wine"[38] (which was expensive and rare). The total membership of the church was estimated to be thirty thousand between 1948 and 1968.

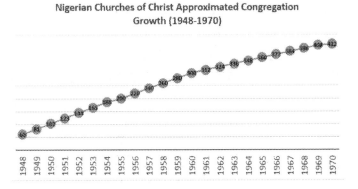

Figure 6

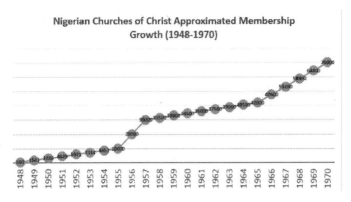

Figure 7

Approximate estimated church population growth

Why was the church growing so fast, and why did it continue to grow and impact the lives of people dramatically in subsequent years? The reason was that the message encompassed teaching and encouraging the following:

- Have dependence on God's Word, the Bible, as a divine and authoritative instrument, rather than human thoughts and doctrines.
- Recognize the inerrant nature of the scriptures.
- God's judgment is profoundly wiser and better than what humankind can offer.
- God's sacrifice of his Son for the salvation of humankind far exceeds whatever humans have to give.

- There are no visible earthly headquarters from which power emanates; it comes from God through the scriptures. Christ is the head of the church, and where the head is dwells the headquarters.

- Money raised within the local congregation is not funneled to any earthly headquarters, other than for local evangelistic benevolent work.

- Selected or appointed local leaders, where there are no elders, assume the administrative overseeing and daily supervision of the church.

These issues were appealing to the people, which contributed to their receptivity. Horton saw, as a primary concern, the need to equip men for preaching, develop church leaders, and tackle ethical problems. There were also doctrinal issues, and "the new churches needed maturing. Unfortunately," he said, "they did not have the personnel to meet these needs and challenges."[39] When Horton was asked how he intended to meet these challenges, he said, "In less than two months we began a three-month Bible training class for men who wanted to preach. After each class (from 8:00 a.m. to 4:00 p.m.), we went out almost every day to villages, marketplaces, church buildings, etc., for preaching and in question-and-answer sessions, on weekends, the students were urged to visit places where they could teach, knowing these prospective students were untrained in public speaking or preaching."[40] This was a good experiment for them to get their feet wet.

They were neophytes and had to be like a mother bird, helping its brood to make their first flight. They were to teach whatever they learned, and the zeal of these men, both young and old, who were discovering biblical concepts, led them to a continually expanding outreach.

At this stage of the work, "Almost all efforts were directed towards outreach and utilizing biblical concepts and teachings as our creed. This concept was perhaps, not new nor taught and emphasized in Nigeria, we felt dependence on God's words alone was fully adequate."[41]

Because of the issues affecting the movement, Horton was asked some of the factors that were detrimental to or that impeded the Nigerian evangelistic work. He mentioned the following:

- lack of in-depth knowledge of the Bible
- entrenched denominational practices.
- entrenched pagan beliefs and practices.
- ethical problems and a deep sense of loyalty or lack thereof
- sectional rivalry or tribal cleavages and jealousies.

He spent considerable time on Bible instruction, but he also conducted individual and group counseling on various problems affecting the churches. He was unrelenting in nurturing and encouraging preachers, whom he said were a great influence in establishing churches. When he returned from the United States in 1953, C. A. O. Essien told him that there were 185 churches in Nigeria, resulting from the influence and teaching of the trained preachers.

The issues on the establishment and management of schools and hospitals were a recurring theme. He "postponed these activities until others could be persuaded to join in the work" and could not allow them to detract from evangelism, which was of paramount importance and the central focus of his mission. He also found that with American support to Nigerians "came abuses, which most American churches could not understand as some Nigerians were motivated by unworthy motives." He gave heart-searching contemplation to the difficulty of finding "a balance for misinformed support and selfish motivation."[42]

The evils of American support to Nigerian churches and preachers were many. Horton said that Nigerian churches could become dependent and would neglect assuming their responsibilities to the preachers; consequently, they would not be motivated to sponsor world evangelism. Additionally, support from America could make (and has made) many Nigerian evangelists materialistic. "Support from America can lose their proper relation to the Nigerian churches."[43]

Horton's tenacity in his approach and vision on what the church should be in Nigeria, as it was in the New Testament, could never be argued. He kept a straight path in pursuing and maintaining a systematic approach, determining the direction of the church in Nigeria. His work was not confined only to administrative duties; preaching and teaching were the bread and butter of his mission. Each day, he was observed attending to appointments in villages, where he taught in public places, village council huts, and denominational church buildings.

As Reda Goff reports in *The Great Nigerian Mission*:

> "We prepared a large chart of all the churches and with the native preachers planned a schedule by which each congregation would be visited for a meeting occasionally by the evangelists. The men began their meeting on a Sunday and preached morning and evening and from house to house for ten days. Then they visit their homes for three days and pass to the next appointment to begin on a Sunday again. Some time they go into a new area where the people have requested to hear the gospel. New congregations have resulted. Sometimes they discover

a congregation which has departed from the gospel. Errors have been corrected, and congregation revealed as being hopelessly in error. These evangelists have baptized an average of about 300 souls each month since this schedule of work began."[44]

Ukpom Bible Training College

As the churches increased numerically, the need for intensive, long-term training of faithful young men became apparent. Short-term courses were brief, and information gleaned was limited in scope. Any expansion of evangelical thrust depended on the caliber of the messenger's education and the extent to which he could articulate intelligently biblical principles and doctrines. The church was rapidly entering a stage in which denominational religionists would use their weight to crush ill-prepared evangelists. Acquisition of advanced academic knowledge would enable one to gain a better grasp of his subject matter and gain respectability. Insistence on better training was common among the preachers and churches; church leaders agitated for long-term Bible studies. They would not relent in their plea for the missionaries to establish and manage schools. The missionaries who were not prepared for the magnitude of the work and the great potential ultimately yielded, realizing what they would need to sustain the work. On August 11, 1953, Howard Horton interrupted his work to confer with the leaders in Nashville, Tennessee, regarding the following:

- the need for more white missionaries
- support for additional native preachers
- a resident training school for young interns preparing to enter the ministry.
- the management of the secular village schools

In making his appeal to the brethren in Nashville, he felt like Rev. Nathaniel Boocock of the Methodist Mission, who also—and much earlier than Horton— had expressed, "We shall have to train them, and train them carefully and long, and I know of no better means of doing so than by the wise use of such a training institution."[45]

Howard flew back to Nigeria, much encouraged to initiate new plans and programs. It was in September 1953 that "we saw the beginning of the realization of some of the things we had dreamed and prayed for with all of our hearts. Since then, things have happened so rapidly that we can hardly believe that it is true. We can only thank our Father."[46] While the needs for expenses and materials were being processed, Lawrence Avenue decided to jump-start, by faith, the training. Vultee

Boulevard Church in Nashville also rendered assistance. Two hundred copies of J. D. Cox's book on church history were furnished by the Sherrod Avenue Church in Florence, Alabama.

In 1955, a fifty-five-year land lease was signed between members of the board of trustees of the church—consisting of Howard Horton, Jimmy Johnson, and Eugene Peden—and Ukpom village chiefs. This was also the year (1953) when an event of profound proportion occurred. Lucien and Ida Palmer, with their two children, Eddie and Patsy, arrived in Nigeria as missionaries. Upon receiving the historic news about the recognition of the Church of Christ, Palmer wrote to Lawrence Avenue Church, "Congratulations to all of us! We have been notified and have received official papers to the effect that we have been fully registered with the government of Nigeria. This is a long sought-for recognition by the church and I am sure all of us rejoice greatly over the accomplishment."[47] Then Palmer explained the Certificate of Incorporation, number 387, dated July 23, 1955: "This document entitles the church to an immediate benefit, the receiving of grant-in aids for secular Christian Schools managed by the missionaries."[48]

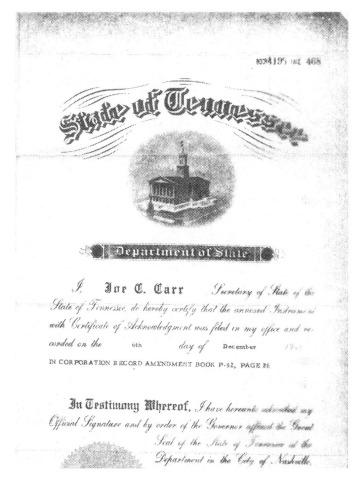

Figure 8

Certificate of incorporation in

Nashville, Tennessee, USA

Two years later, a similar event took place in Nashville, the acquisition of registered status as a nonprofit organization became imperative. The need to register African Christian Schools as a legally constituted body in the US, and the Nigerian Mission Trustees in Nigeria, each operating separately without duplicating their services. African Christian Schools was purposely for raising funds and recruiting personnel from America, while the Nigerian Mission Trustees protected and represented the churches in legal matters and encouraged all secular and religious matters in Nigeria.

It would be unrealistic to contemplate establishing schools and hospitals through funds raised directly from the church, as funds could not be easily attained among Churches of Christ for that purpose. In a hierarchical organized system, however, this is obtainable. Doctrinally and administratively, among the Churches of Christ, each church is autonomous, independent of each other, yet they cooperate to sponsor evangelistic programs. They also respond cooperatively to both national and international disasters and embark on medical missions in areas where benevolence is needed. Howard Horton observed that nowhere in America could a gospel preacher be given such an opportunity for directing the spiritual life of the next generation—again, except in denominal churches.

As enticing as the unique opportunity was, the idea of establishing a two-year biblical program, where students paid no fees at the Bible school, sparked additional problems for the missionaries. The arduous burden of feeding students who had no financial backing meant dependence on American churches. Responding to this challenge, Howard Horton, the spiritual architect of the school, thought that a long period of training posed another problem. Poverty is almost universal here. During a three months' course, I saw men without adequate food; one man was without food for at least two days before I learned of it. This made it clear that we could not expect the young men to remain with us for two years without some means of obtaining necessary food.[49]

Fund solicitation from sister congregations was immediate and urgent, and the positive response from many congregations was encouraging. R. B. Sweat, an ardent supporter of the Nigerian work, solicited the ten-dollars-per-student budget through the weight of his media publication; he also donated needed study materials.

Prior to the signing of the fifty-five-year land-lease agreement between the Church of Christ trustees and Ukpom village chiefs, including the surrounding villages, they jointly built a temporary thatched-mud and extremely damp dormitory for students, as a gesture of cooperation and gratitude. The land-lease agreement and the construction of apartments began in August 1954. Initially, the administrators had no idea of the overwhelming number of candidates who desired to attend the school, nor did they anticipate it. Most did not fully realize the scope or the goal, beyond redeeming, reclaiming, and retaining lost souls and, above all, helping to expand the borders of the kingdom. The school was not to provide a general secular education that would translate to better job opportunities and positions. At first, sixty-seven candidates applied.

The opening ceremony on February 1, 1954, was an unprecedented, jubilant occasion that attracted many in high government positions. Chiefs, church leaders, and villagers descended on the campus to celebrate the formal opening of the Bible school. Thus was another milestone in the history of the church destined to change the lives of millions of people in Nigeria and beyond.

Not much was done to advertise for students, except verbal contacts to all known churches. The result for prospective students was alarming, giving the administrators' ample opportunity to select emotionally stable, academically qualified students. At the end of the two-year training program, of the seventy-two candidates who applied for admission, forty-two graduated.

Effiong Moses Akpan	Solomon P. Aquaowo	Effiong F. Ating
John Akpan	E. E. Asuquo	Effiong John Ebong
Udo Essien Akpan	Etim Asuquo	S. T. Ebong
Udo Joe Akpan	Akpan Jackson Attat	S. W. Ebong
		Asuquo A. Effiong

Archibong E. Ekanem

Eyo Okon Ekanem

Sunday A. Ekanem

S. U. E. Ekanem

Tom U. Ekpo

Peter Uko Eno

Oyong Jacob

Enyenihi

Ekitmfin A. Equere

Antai Esang

Etim John Esin

Essien Akpan Essien

E. O. Essien

Friday A. Essien

Okon E. Essien

E.O. Essien

Friday E. Essien

S.I. Essien

E. A. U. Etok

Solomon U.U. Etok

Isong T. Etukudo

Willie Etukudo

Eyo Umana Eno

D. O. Ibekwe

Okocie Ibeukumere

D. A. Inyang

T. A. Inyang

Etim Udo Inyang

Udo Inyang

James O.K. Iregbu

Kelser Udo Ituk Lawrence

Matthew Job

Moses I. Nwankwo

Asuquo O. Odohoefre

Edet Odokwo Akaiso

Chukwu Oguwru

Reginald Okereke

Esuabana E. Okon

Edet O. Ononokpono

Ikpe E. Otoro

Eno O. Otoyo

I. I. Stephen

Etim Wilson Udo

Okona Etefia Udo

Etim Alexander Udorung

Joseph Ukagwu

Okon Stephen Udofia

Ezekiel I. Umanah

Effiong Moses

Akpan Harry

T. Umanah

N. R. Umana

Okon E. Umoh

Raphael Edet William

Etukudo Isong

Etukudo

Hillary U. Akpakpan

T. C. Akpadiaha

Erik Anyonwu

(Students names provided by Dr. Timothy Akpakpan of Ukpom Bible College, Ukpom, Abak)

As Lucien Palmer recognized quickly upon his arrival, the Ukpom Bible Training School held the key to the future stability and expansion of the church in Nigeria. The curriculum embraced by Ukpom Bible Training College (UBTC) comprised an in-depth study of the Old and New Testaments, including the following:

- systematic study of church history
- scheme of redemption
- acts of the apostles
- epistles and book of Revelation
- study of denominations
- the history and departure from the faith
- preparation and delivery of sermons
- the science of hermeneutics

The students' first trial, in exercising their knowledge, ability, and love of the scriptures, in engaging the religious world, besides serving in congregations without preachers, came in 1954. The first-year students went on their internships to various localities: Calabar, Akpabuyo, Oron, Eket, Abak, Ikot Ekpene, and Aba. Upon graduation in 1955, this same group dispersed to Lagos, Aba, Abak, Utu Etim Ekpo, Etinan, Eket, Oron, Ikot Nakanda, Atimbo, Creek Town, Okoyong, Itu, Ibiono, and the then–Midwestern State, now Warri. Below is the picture of the graduates of Ukpom Bible School in 1955:

Howard Horton's Role

When I asked Howard Horton, in a telephone interview on October 21, 1998, about his role, he said, "I saw this first essential as an immediate beginning of Bible training to equip men for preaching first principles of the gospel. There were doctrinal and ethical problems; the new congregations needed nurturing." When I asked how he tackled some of the problems they encountered, he said, "First, in less than three months, we began a three-month training class for men who wanted to preach. After classes, 8:00 a.m.–4:00 p.m., we went almost every day to village marketplaces, church buildings, for preaching; there were question-and-answer sessions."[50]

In January 1954, the first-year students started classes in the temporary, damp, mud classroom erected by Ukpom village. The present classroom block and residence for the Palmers, funded by Vultee Church of Christ in Nashville, was completed in August 1955. On July 23, 1955, the church received the federal government's Certificate of Incorporation.

While Horton's role gradually and voluntarily diminished from intensive evangelical outreach to administrative duties, Jimmy Johnson assumed the supervision needed on construction. Eugene Peden preached in open forums and established approximately eighty congregations within a short period.

In the first four months of his arrival, Peden baptized 752. At the end of one year, Peden had baptized nearly 1,500 and started 15 new congregations. In 1958, Peden wrote, "I already have preached 321 sermons this year. This has meant traveling about 30,000 miles [on bad, potholed bush roads and paths].

Eugene Peden further wrote, "I have also taught 350 Bible classes in the Calabar province and in Iboland."[51] His energy and zeal for lost souls was unequaled; preachers gave him the nickname "the man of steel."

Brother C. A. O. Essien, on his own, between 1948 and 1952, trained a small band of preachers in the three-month Bible courses, as well as support groups—men who coordinated teaching and preaching appointments that resulted in the establishment of sixty churches, with an approximate membership of seven hundred. From 1952 to 1962, after the first four missionaries—Howard Johnson, Jimmy Johnson, Eugene Peden, and Lucien Palmer—arrived the country, there were approximately thirty-five thousand converted Christians, in areas that Wendell Broom's document in his unpublished document: Church of Christ Among the Ibibio, 1970, described as *Ibibio*. The designation Ibibio, geopolitically, includes only a small section of the area. The people of the Old Cross River Region, such as Calabar (Efik, with a universally accepted written language), Annang, Ibeno, and Oron, with their peculiar and indistinguishable dialects, were lumped into what Broom called Ibibio.

Regardless, Broom's statistical assumptions composed of Ibibio excluded Igbos, River State (Bendel), Onitcha, Owerri, Enugu, Nsukka, Lagos, and Ibadan. Other area's churches in these regions were growing at higher rates than the Ibibio, and the size of the areas not enumerated were more than ten times greater than the Ibibio, Efik, Annang, and Oron enclaves. By Nigeria's sheer population and size, churches flourished at parallel levels to the Efik Ibibio rate. Once the Bible Training Schools; the Nigerian Christian Bible College, Ukpom, Abak; Onicha Ngwa Bible College; and the Nigerian Christian Hospital were established, these institutions provided the impetus and opportunities for outreach evangelism.

P-12, PAGE 14

BOOK 4195 PAGE 489

AMENDMENT TO CHARTER OF INCORPORATION

At a Meeting of the Board of Directors of

Nigeria Christian Schools Foundation, Inc.
Name of Corporation

duly held at the office of said corporation in ____Nashville, Tennessee____, on the _____ day of

_____, 19____, the following resolution was adopted, its advisability declared and a meeting
directors
of the stockholders duly called to vote thereon, which resolution is as follows:

To change the name of said corporation from Nigeria Christian

Schools Foundation, Inc. to African Christian Schools Foundation, Inc.,

and to amend the Charter of Incorporation accordingly, and to further

amend the charter to show that the purpose of said corporation is for

establishing, maintaining, and operating Christian elementary and high

schools and colleges, to provide spiritual and secular education and to

offer benevolent and medical assistance in all of Africa rather than in

Nigeria, West Africa only. Specifically, the original charter shall be

amended to show (1) that the name of the corporation is now African

Christian Schools Foundation, Inc.; and (2) that the purpose of said

African Christian Schools Foundation, Inc. is to provide spiritual and

secular education and to offer benevolent and medical assistance in

Africa and for establishing, maintaining, and operating Christian ele-

mentary and high schools and colleges in which the Bible is taught, along

with academic studies in Africa and to continue to operate the schools

already established and to solicit funds for the operation thereof.

Figure 10

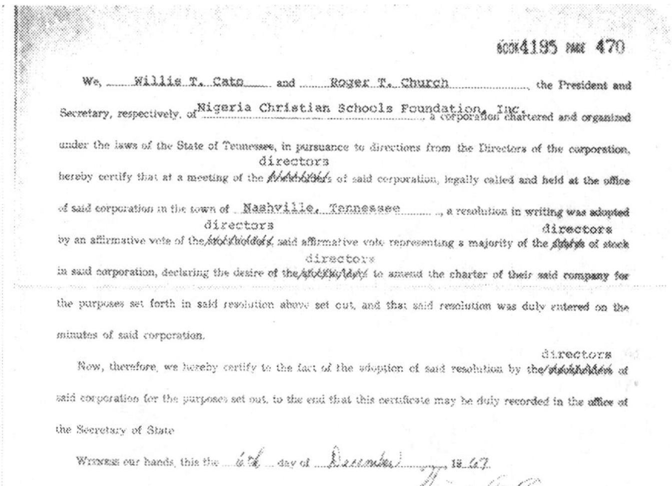

BOOK 4195 PAGE 470

We, Willie T. Cato and Roger T. Church, the President and Secretary, respectively, of Nigeria Christian Schools Foundation, Inc. a corporation chartered and organized under the laws of the State of Tennessee, in pursuance to directions from the Directors of the corporation, hereby certify that at a meeting of the directors of said corporation, legally called and held at the office of said corporation in the town of Nashville, Tennessee, a resolution in writing was adopted by an affirmative vote of the directors said affirmative vote representing a majority of the directors of stock in said corporation, declaring the desire of the directors to amend the charter of their said company for the purposes set forth in said resolution above set out, and that said resolution was duly entered on the minutes of said corporation.

Now, therefore, we hereby certify to the fact of the adoption of said resolution by the directors of said corporation for the purposes set out, to the end that this certificate may be duly recorded in the office of the Secretary of State.

Witness our hands, this the 6th day of December, 1967.

President or Vice-President

Secretary or Asst. Secretary

STATE OF TENNESSEE

COUNTY OF Davidson

Personally appeared before me, a Notary Public of the county aforesaid, Willie T. Cato and Roger T. Church with whom I am personally acquainted and who made oath before me in due form of law that Willie T. Cato is the president and Roger T. Church is the Secretary of Nigeria Christian Schools Foundation, Inc. and that the statements made in the foregoing certificate are true.

Witness my hand and official seal at office in Nashville Tennessee, this 6th day of December, 1967.

Figure 11

Certificate of Incorporation, Nashville, Tennessee

Howard Horton, who left the country in December 1954, was replaced by Lucien Palmer. On August 6, 1955, Eugene Peden returned to America, thus ending an epoch of great evangelistic outreach. Howard Horton, James Johnson, and Eugene Peden were men of immense personal convictions, men who were imbued with the Spirit of God and demonstrated unequaled capacities for the general good of God's kingdom. As the years rolled by, many other missionaries, like Lucien Palmer, who administered the Bible school for some time, and Burney Baughman were still insufficient to tackle the volume of work reposed on them. The few new arrivals minimally reduced their workload.

Another unique missionary was John Beckloff. He edited the *Christian Chronicle* while working with the African Christian Schools Foundation in Nashville. John Beckloff arrived in Nigeria on February 7, 1961, along with his wife, Dottie, and their children.

Although no one could have predicted it, and although time and place are not guaranteed to anyone, John ultimately would be buried in Nigeria. If longevity of service for a cause and in a foreign country is worthy of recognition, his burial at Ukpom is a testament to his devotion and to the work for which he devoted his life. John Beckloff saw many missionaries come and go during the years of his epochal service in Nigeria.

As a mark of honor and respect, when Beckloff died, the chiefs and people of Ukpom pleaded that—like Mary Slessor, who was buried in Okoyong, a village not too far from Ikot Usen—John Beckloff be buried at Ukpom, where he spent more time than most of the Church of Christ missionaries; he was buried there. He learned the ways of the people and ate their food.

Many people fail to recognize that in order to survive while attempting to transform the lives of the people into the image of Christ, a missionary had to make sacrifices and to adjust his lifestyle, especially when there was little support. Beckloff lived under the constraint of limited physical conditions but shared all he had with the people. He was loved for these attributes and for his work.

Work beyond the Cross River (The Great Dispersion)

Brother C. A. O. Essien's work expanded beyond mainland Calabar into Akpabuyo, Ikot Nakanda, and Esighi, where thirteen villages accepted the gospel and over a thousand souls were converted. In 1954, some of the graduates of the Ukpom Bible School conducted their internship program among these congregations, and at the end of the internship service, the reports of the forty men positively glowed over the number of people who had turned their lives to Christ. During this period, C. A. O. Essien led a team of students to Ghana, while Brother Wendell Broom went to the Cameroons.

Leadership Training (Stabilizing the Churches)

As the church grew, the demands for advanced long-term training in the scriptures became imperative. Nigerian Christians realized the need to be better equipped for service. They desired raising the standard of living in an environment where preachers were barely remunerated for their service in any of the existing congregations.

Education is an indispensable tool, a weapon to counteract ignorance. It opens one's mind to the world of literature and a world of activism in the social, political, and economic arena, which enables the individual to participate as a servant of God actively and effectively. Serving and knowing God will enhance or lead to loving him, for a person cannot love God without knowing the requirement of his/her duty to God in a complex socio-egalitarian society.

Eighteenth-century English poet Alexander Pope once wrote, "Drink deep, or taste not the Pierian spring."[52] A little learning can lead to vain conviction, causing one to assume that he/she already knows, thereby developing a closed mind. A better knowledge on any subject has the advantage of humbling a truly devoted servant of God; on the other hand, it can make a person haughty and egotistical.

Many from Ukpom sought advanced training in American Christian institutions. The Bible schools at Ukpom and Onicha Ngwa were rudimentary and inadequate, without books, library, teachers, or accommodation to meet advanced academic exercises. There was an undercurrent of dissension among some of the American missionaries as to the wisdom of sponsoring any Nigerian for advanced training in the United States. The Nigerians perceived that the vacuum created by the departure of American missionaries would be filled by anyone, particularly those who had selfish purposes, rather than those with genuine interest in returning to the country to serve after their training.

While we were driving from Onicha Ngwa to Ukpom, Abak, with Brother Bill Curry and his wife, Mary Lou, they introduced the persistent discussion among the missionaries on the wisdom of recommending academically qualified, faithful, and deserving Nigerian Christians for study in any Christian college or university in the United States. Little did we know that the issue was a common discussion topic among American brethren. A few of the brethren were unwilling, others were reluctant, and for others, it was a phobic reaction against helping, thereby igniting further controversy among the races.

Naturally, our views were contrary to their beliefs, especially having just returned from a six-year college program at Southwestern Christian College and Pepperdine University. Bill and Mary Lou Curry became strong allies in advocating sponsoring the training of Nigerian Christians abroad. The American brethren who were in an advantageous position to recommend and sponsor Nigerian Christians reticence or refused did so. The Nigerians felt the Nigerian Christians would, in time, find their way to American universities, regardless. It would be to the detriment of the missionaries and the Nigerian churches to overlook, ignore, or discourage the Nigerian preachers' entry into the United States.

At this stage, the die was cast, and Bill and Mary Lou Curry returned to the fold (the current resident Americans) to champion the cause for encouraging Nigerian Christians to study abroad. Later, they retreated to face reality on the wisdom and benefits of an advanced education for the people. Brother Stephen Okoronkwo and Timothy Akpakpan were, at the time, qualified Christians being discussed; thankfully, they were accorded the opportunity and sponsorship to study abroad. Unfortunately, though, Brother Udo Moses Akpan, a brilliant cum laude–quality student at the Nigerian Christian Secondary School, was not favored, due to relational cleavages. Thankfully, Udo Udo Moses wound up in the USA on his own to acquire his doctorate degree.

Brother Okon E. Mkpong's situation was different, without any obstacles. It appeared that the brethren could no longer discourage Nigerian Christians from pursuing advanced education, which ultimately was advantageous to the church and nation. Brother Nelson Isonguyo also was waiting in the wings to venture into the land of great promise and opportunities.

One hardly understood the logic for discouraging Nigerian Christians from studying in America. Any reason against it was purely conjectural, speculative, and untenable, even though the social ramifications of cultural differences pinged greatly against the American nation and particularly against churches. Edet Essien's case was different. His resources were limited or nonexistent, yet he had the potential and could pursue advanced educational training. While teaching at the Nigerian Christian Secondary School, where I was the principal, he sought a scholarship from our agency, African Christian Schools, and was denied. The village petitioned for him, guaranteeing that when the village harvested the seasonal palm fruit collection—the only reliable source of income for the village—whatever the amount we loaned him would be refunded.

Our organization's refusal to advance Edet Essien the amount needed was devastating, knowing the implication to the future of the mission efforts and the community. Although I was not authorized to do so, I was compelled to take from the sale from the school's resources that Edet Essien needed and loaned it to Edet until the village, as promised and guaranteed, repaid the amount. As expected, I was reprimanded for my unilateral decision to lend the money. With gratitude, the village accepted the conditions and later repaid the money on time.

When Brother Edet Essien returned from the United States, he was a voice of reason, compassionate and energetic in dispensing his Christian duties with pride and honor. The lingering thought remained: why wouldn't the brethren openly encourage Nigerians, without reservation, to study in American Christian universities? Was the reticence or blind refusal due to a lack of money, as they realized their programs were funded through contributions from individual members or congregations?

Most of the churches at the time, by their doctrine and interpretation of the scriptures, would not sponsor benevolent or secular educational pursuits. Did they fear, due to the pathological, discriminatory racial environment in which they were raised, that if they dared discount or trample on their racial upbringing, it would backfire on their work, and they might be withdrawn from the work they loved? The environment does play a vital role in the responses in most situations the missionaries, as good as most of them were, suffered from their parents' sour-grapes syndrome—the age-old prejudice, a learned behavior that saw other racial groups as inferior, as second-class humans, or perhaps afraid they would want to marry their white women. As they provided the skills the students needed to know about the learning process, the missionaries marveled at the students' abilities to assimilate or synthesize concepts.

Figure 12

The first graduates of the Ukpom Bible
College, Ukpom, Abak, 1955, with some
of the missionaries and their families
L–R: C. A. O. Essien, Eugene Peden, Lucien
Palmer, Howard Horton, and Elvis Huffard

CHAPTER 4

Foot Soldier Movement

Nigeria is linguistically diverse with a reasonable degree of sophistication and fluency in English language. Many learned English beginning from the first two or three years of primary school. In villages and in large cosmopolitan cities, like Aba, Owerri, Enugu, Lagos, Ibadan, Abakaliki, and Calabar, or in some of the northern Muslim states, the language spoken are mostly the local language of the tribes. The adulterated pidgin English, which is common especially in government offices and for trading purposes is also spoken. The native dialects, Hausa in the North; Yoruba in the West; Igbo, Efik Ibibio, English, and pidgin English in the South, are used, depending on which one is common or appropriate.

In 1948, in Ikot Usen, where the church started, C. A. O. Essien's foot soldiers, some on bicycles; a few on foot—went to many communities. Before Ukpom, Abak, the church was started at Manta, Abak, and Nelson R. Umana was one of Brother C. A. O. Essien's first converts and students. Ukpom, Abak, is unique because of its prominence as the village in which the first advanced biblical training school was established in 1954. The church was converted, en masse, from the Nazarene church, with Brother Samuel M. Essien, a colleague of C. A. O. Essien. The mass conversion of the Nazarene church leaders and their members led to the acquisition of one the largest concrete church buildings in the area. This congregation was plagued by major controversies, one of which was polygamy. This, of course, was no surprise among those who converted to the church. In time, as they waded through the concept and practice of polygamy, many readily changed—some reluctantly, perhaps. Due to the stringent economic conditions, they capitulated in favor of a monogamous lifestyle.

Ukpom's prominence as the first Church of Christ in Abak evolved by default, leading to events at Manta and Midim. Brother C. A. O. Essien, because of his association with people in Manta and Midim, conducted several Bible classes that included people like Ukpekpe of Ikot Ayan and Ntuk of Ikot Mbon Ikono, Uyo, who also visited Chief Solomon Udo (Udo Adiaha of Midim), Waterside, Abak. After several Bible classes, Chief Solomon, his family, and his neighbors—Robert Umoren, Job Johnson, Bassey James, and Sunday James—opted to be converted. The missionaries at Ikot Usen were invited; maybe the excitement of the American brethren's visit also brought the problem of where to host them.

Dr. Timothy Akpakpan reported that Chief Solomon Udo approached the Nazarene church at Midim, where there was the only permanent large building, to host the visitors. When the appointed day came, keys to the Nazarene church building disappeared; some members of the Nazarene church, who were hostile and opposed to the church establishment in the community, hid the keys of the Nazarene church building. The Church of Christ leaders were embarrassed, disgraced, and disappointed.

The disappointment prompted Chief Solomon to donate his property at Adaha Anya in 1951 for the erection of a wattle-mud church building. He then approached his uncle, the paramount ruler Chief Udo Ekong, who, upon hearing of the dastardly behavior of his subjects, exercised his prerogative and requested a meeting with the missionaries. The meeting with Chief Udo Ekong resulted in a promise to the missionaries of land to establish a missionary outpost in the area.

As an offshoot of these events, two churches emerged; first, from Manta, Okon Udofia, Sampson Akpan, and Umanah R. Umanah established a place at Ikot Oku Ubo, in Michael Udo Udo's residence. The second group met at the Christ Army Church in Isaac Udo Offiong's compound. In 1962, Evangelist Ukpekpe converted the membership of Christ Army Church to Church of Christ. In 1963, the two churches merged. Later, an event of greater significance for the churches was the merger of the Manta and Midim churches; both congregations exhibited great maturity and love. The ideal location was Manta junction, where both villages are contiguously bound.

Oron Movement

Religious groups like the Roman Catholics, the Baptists, and especially the Primitive Methodist Church tended to feel they had a monopoly in the territory. These groups were the first missionaries to set foot in the area. They intimidated those they knew had become members or who contemplated leaving their churches. Some of their members were abrasive in their characterization of the church. Regardless of the initial refusal of Church of Christ children to enroll in denominational schools or to receive immediate medical care, such denials became a catalyst that energized Church of Christ members to hold firmly to their views and doctrine.

It is true the denominational churches leaped further, having permeated Oron communities, for example, with schools and hospitals. Professor O. E. Uya cited Reverend W. J. Ward as saying that every established mission had at least three clearly defined departments of service, the educational, the medical, and the definitely religious." In pursuing these objectives by the Methodist, E. A. Ayandele opined that the Methodist schools were built by the missionaries primarily for producing catechists, deacons, and priests. This became the precedence that justified the establishment of educational institutions for the Methodist Mission.

Mary Slesssor, (the Queen of Okoyong) the earliest Anglican Mission missionary to Calabar, remarked that "...schools were the instrument that enhanced church growth. She added that, schools and teaching go with the gospel. Further, she taught that you cannot have one without the other, as confirmed by Bacil Milkler, who wrote that Mary Slesssor always carried medicine for the sick bodies as well as Christ's medicine for their sin-sick souls."[53]

Though the infusion of denominations had enormous sway on the people, pantheistic beliefs and practices were not far behind. Pantheism was steeped in the psyche of the people. The church, then, had to wage battle with false religious practices and cultural paganistic beliefs.

Educationally, the denominations were far advanced, with schools that were well established. They had more trained personnel for their mission centers and for recruitment in government services. Socially, all those who became Church of Christ members were communicants of one religious group or the other. There was no direct distinction between the school and one's religion or church, as these were wedded together.

In 1951, Effiong Atte Enyenihi, who was the first convert of the Church of Christ, studied under C. A. O. Essien, who visited Enyenihi's home village, Oyubia,

Oron. "A handful of individuals were persuaded to study with him, according to Brother Bassey Oboho's pamphlet.[54] In the document on the advent of the church in the village, Oboho wrote that they "were received with mixed feelings, vis-à-vis the community that resolved not to permit any other church on their soil except the Methodist."[55]

Asuquo Essang Enyenihi, Eyo Afahaesuhe, Effiong F. Ating, Asuquo Odohoefre, Sunday Okwong Enyenihi, Edet Ekpo Uno, Mma (Madam) Ikwo Asuquo Essang, and Chief Asuquo Ewa Oboho—Brother Bassey Oboho's pamphlet stated that these were the first converts who were baptized at Udim Entghe Amba.

These members began to seek recognition and property for their worship place. Some Methodist elite, particularly Mr. Robert Odohoefre, were still dissatisfied and often openly derisive. Openly using expletives, they asked Chief Henry N. Enyenihi not to grant the visiting missionaries an audience or permission to establish at Oyubia. Chief Henry Enyenihi was, at the time, one of the most industrious and prominent officers of the then-administrative offices in Eket, Ubium, Okobo, and Oron.

During Chief Enyenihi's siesta, he overheard noises outside his room. The message was delivered to him, persuading him not to accommodate the Church of Christ missionaries. Without flinching, the chief, in his wisdom, told his dissenting members not to stand in God's way and to allow the Church of Christ members to preach and to settle in the village. Thus, came a tacit recognition and approval for Howard Horton and Wendell Broom to share their message to the crowd of villagers in the village shed.

In 1952, the missionaries, in cooperation with Brother C. A. O. Essien, sent a young, intelligent, knowledgeable evangelist, Brother Robin N. Umana, to settle in Oyubia. Soon after his arrival, the church picked up momentum, growing by leaps and bounds, and I was one of his converts in 1953. Brother Bassey Oboho wrote, The tenure of Evangelist Umana service at Oyubia was eventful because he fast-tracked soul winning and inculcated in the young church, sound doctrine. It was during one of the evangelism trips to Oyubia, during Robin Umana's preaching, that Brother C. A. O. Essien asked to be baptized at Esuk Oron River. (Although, for four years, he had learned and taught and had baptized many, he was never baptized until he requested it.) They obliged and baptized him.

For several months, the initial members met in the bedroom apartment of Effiong Atte Enyenihi and later took residence on the veranda of Asuquo Essang. Brother "Eyo Afahaesuhe also quartered the evangelist."[56] Chief Asuquo Ewa Oboho gave about three pieces of land for the construction of the church building. The Oyubia church became the springboard for churches at Oruko, Ikpe Oro, Oron Town, Okossi, Nsie, and Utine.

The Oruko church was the second congregation established in the area in 1952. Oron Town, because of its urban nature, needed a mature evangelist who was experienced in the scriptures, someone who was patient and ready to absorb the punishing blows of opposition. Brother Augustine U. Oyo, a leading member of Forty Stadium Road Church of Christ, wrote that the attempt to establish a congregation in Oron Urban started as far back as 1957, by an indigent Okon Otoyo and the late Brother Etim John Esin in the village of Esin Ufot. Since the inhabitants of the area were hostile to the truth, coupled with other mitigating factors, like lack of committed men with accommodation for worship, their effort did not see the light of day.

In 1962, Brother Oyo wrote,

> "A fresh team of missionaries came from Cross River State with the same sound doctrine message. These new arrivals settled in a house on Ebito Street. A few converts were made, but they soon slid back into the world, especially because there were no visionary leaders."[57]

The struggle to establish a church continued through the early part of the Nigerian Civil War in 1967. Brother Oyo later stated that some of the surviving members "re-emerged and gathered at Azikiwe Street in a brother's house." Many members, like Edet Duncan, Bassey George Ekpo, and Minister Etim Robert Offiong, were the early pillars of the church who banded together to procure land for the construction of their thatched church building, for which the church had a permanent location in 1972.

With the leadership of Brother Etim R. Offiong and with E. D. Bassey supervising the construction, the foundation of their permanent building was laid in 1990. This congregation was one of the first to support its preacher full time—inadequately but understandably, due to the economic conditions of the time. The Oron Town congregation had a succession of faithful and committed ministers who patiently labored in the congregation for long periods. One of these preachers was Brother Amana Abidiak, and the church experienced tremendous growth in many areas, like purposeful planned giving, benevolence, and active participatory evangelism by every member. Brother Oyo shared the fact that because many of their members were destitute, they spent more on benevolence.

The focus of the congregation, more than anything else, was evangelism as a method to share the eternal truth and God's blessing. They sponsored the work at Ebughu, Unyehe, in Mbo Local Government Areas, and Udung Uko LGA, where many were persuaded to accept the teachings of the New Testament.

I had interpreted for Brother Nicks often in 1955; this time, the trip was different. He informed me that morning, as we drove, that he had received the horrific and sad news that his father, a respected and reputable song leader in the brotherhood, had been killed in a car accident on his way to a congregation, where he was to lead the song service in a gospel meeting. Nicks taught that morning, courageously, without a hint of sadness. As I observed him, however, I felt that his outward appearance was not reflective of his mind construction. He bore the loss graciously and, indeed, with dignity. In 1956, he moved to Onicha Ngwa, where he lived until 1956. He returned to Nigeria on June 12 for the second time to see the people and the work for which he had made numerous sacrifices.

Conventionally, in the Efik, Igbo, or Yoruba primary languages, one would translate each pattern of thought and expression into the language spoken and understood by the people. These conditions were decisively conducive to determining the future of the school in the area where Igbo is spoken, unlike Efik-Ibibio, which is spoken among the Efik Ibibio villages. This helped designers to consider recruiting students in areas where teachers and preachers would translate biblical literature and textual information into the thought pattern of the local area. Some of the luminaries of the school were Akandu, Onwusoro, Effiong Atte, and Jacob Achinefu, who exerted their energies in teaching and preaching in Igbo. These and other young neophytes developed the ability to understand the scheme of redemption and to interpret it into the language of the area.

In the early 1950s and '60s, the forces that were present when the church started in the Ibibio and Calabar areas were also present and at work in the Igbo areas. The first few converts from Igbo who enrolled at Ukpom Bible Training College became, like an aqueduct, the means to convey the gospel message to their communities. There was strong evidence that Brother C. A. O. Essien had already traversed some of the villages in the Igbo localities. The arrival of missionaries like J. W. Nicks, Rees Bryant, James Finney, Douglas Lawyer, Jim Massey, and Henry Farrar helped to accelerate the establishment and expansion of churches in the Igbo areas. It should be observed, however, that Nicks and Finney were the first American missionaries to live at Onicha Ngwa, when Nicks moved from Ukpom, Abak, in 1957 to Onicha Ngwa.

The success of the evangelistic outreach in Calabar and Ibibio villages motivated the brethren to consider the need to establish a post in the Igbo area. To initiate an evangelistic outpost in the Igbo area, the brethren considered factors such as convenience and proximity of the location to an actively running stream; communication; and access to transportation and a market. Additionally, members reasoned that commuting to Ukpom would be excessively expensive for students; toiling peasants among the young churches could not afford the expense involved. All of these were beyond the capabilities of the churches. Besides, it was felt that though English was the medium of instruction in the schools conversationally, the Igbo language/dialect was universally spoken in Igbo.

Bill Nicks was the first principal of Onicha Ngwa Bible Training College. He returned briefly to America in 1957 to raise needed funds for the construction of the second classroom, but reentered Nigeria in June 1958, where he worked until October 1959. Rees Bryant and his wife, Patti, went home to raise funds to build the second school classroom. They returned to Nigeria in April 1960 for their second missionary tour. Soon, a small nucleus of believers and churches appealed for the duplication of the experiences of Igbo graduates of Ukpom Bible School among the Igbo enclaves. The inconveniences in transportation, the cost-of-living arrangements, and the distance, however, imposed a great burden, beyond the means of the Igbo Christians. Replication of the Ukpom Bible School experience was a necessity as "route to penetrate the Igbo areas with the gospel."[58]

Brother J. W. Nicks, who had arrived in Nigeria in October 1955, spearheaded the possibility of establishing a mission post in the Igbo area. He "learned from letters and articles, sent by Howard Horton and Elvis Huffard Sr., of the need for intensive evangelistic work in Nigeria."[59]

Responding to a questionnaire, Nicks wrote that his "motivation was to obey the Great Commission to 'go into all the world' with the gospel. When I heard there was much receptivity and need in Nigeria, I was ready to do my part to help."[60] Brother Nicks spent October 1955 through 1957, teaching and visiting churches in Ibibio and Efik-Ibibio–speaking congregations. Meanwhile, he conducted intensive outreach in Igboland, preparing the way for eventual residency and assumption of work in Igbo.

Brother Stephen Okoronkwo, a graduate of Ukpom Bible Training College, was of immense assistance as a traveling partner and competent translator for Nicks and other missionaries. He was multilingual; having been born in Arochuku, he spoke his Igbo native tongue, Efik, and English fluently. He was a considerable asset to the cause and much help to Brother Nicks.

While scouting for a suitable location to establish God's work, they were introduced to the then-district officer in Aba, who, learning of Brother Nicks's intention to launch a biblical beachhead in the area, welcomed Brother Nicks with open arms and granted him the former rest house used by officers in court cases. This facility was located eleven miles east of Aba, now in Abia State Local Government Area, toward Ikot Ekpene, of the then-Southeastern State. At the time, the facilities were vacant and "were no longer in use, the church sort of inherited it."[61] Brother Nicks and his wife, Gerry, moved into the rented native courthouse premises until they acquired land and constructed the first mission house on a fifteen-acre property at Ntigha Onicha Ngwa. This house became the initial hospital structure used by Dr. Henry Farrar.

Other game players who contributed immeasurably to the spreading and stabilizing of churches in Igbo, in addition to Brother Stephen Okoronkwo, were Josiah Akandu, Ndukwe, and Reginald Okereke, who were the first second-year students at Onicha Ngwa Bible School. Later, Nicks wrote, "We selected forty prospective students out of a great number who applied for enrollment. These men became great preachers among Igbos, like Jacob Achinefu, Daniel Ogbonna, Reuben Iheanacho, and Chukwu Oguru."[62] Nicks became actively involved in teaching and ministering to the churches at Onicha Ngwa, Nlagu, including Itungwa, Umohia, and Aba.

Nicks estimated that there were already five hundred Christians in about fifteen congregations when they arrived. Nicks and Brother James Finney, with their faithful interpreters, were a great contribution to the establishment of new churches. Prior to this, though, Howard Horton, Elvis Huffard, and Burney Bawcom had settled for about five years at Ikot Usen, Ibiono, penetrating some sections of Igboland, thereby creating a favorable atmosphere for Nicks's incredibly successful evangelistic outreach.

Within a noticeably short time, churches sprang up in many villages; for example, ten churches in Asa-Akoli, Ohanze, and Umuodosi; four in Uzuakoli, in Umuahia, Owerri, and Mbaise, of which one was Ife Nowutu. The scope of evangelistic effort expanded to embrace communities in Enugu, where two churches were also started, including one in Nsukka, as Nicks reported. The initial churches established in Iboland were in Uzuakoli villages, of which Obze was one.

While we were still at Ukpom, we traveled to Onicha Ngwa and Umuodosi to start these churches, but Uzuakoli churches were established by Horton, with Chukwu Ogwuru, David Ibekwe, Josiah Akandu, Josiah Nwadioha, and A. K. Owusoro as interpreters and preachers at various villages. Another Ibo preacher who also graduated from Ukpom Bible College, whose severe asthmatic condition hindered his evangelistic effort, was Moses Nwankwo, He and I traveled together to Uzuakoli with Brother Nicks, teaching in this area.

Figure 13

Onicha Ngwa Bible Training College Students

Like Ukpom Bible School, Onicha Ngwa Bible College (ONBC) was born of necessity to make the school accessible to the Igbo people and to reduce the high cost of transportation for students who came from financially deprived families. It could be said that the establishment of such a school in the area provided a psychological sense of identity within the Igbo communities.

To replicate the Ukpom BTS experience, certain factors were necessary, such as accessibility to a thoroughfare, availability of water, and proximity to a commercial center, south of Aba, eleven miles from the anticipated location of the college. The school would attract students and teachers also from Ikot Ekpene contiguous villages, where numerous churches existed. Another reason that was factored into the search for a suitable location was a communication system. At the time, a telephone system, though still in a primitive state, linked Aba-Ikot Ekpene, Uyo, Oron, Calabar, Oyubia, and Eket. These phone exchange lines were used mostly by government administrative officers, postal officers, private entrepreneurial agents, and some well-established church mission centers. The Onicha Ngwa location was, therefore, unique and inviting.

In March 1957, J. W. Nicks and his family, at their temporary residence, wrote, "We met in the Palaver [court] house before the construction of our school building." [63]

The first group of teachers were Bill Nicks, James Finney, D. D. Isonguyo, and Josiah Akandu, who became very prominent as the protector of the school property during the civil war years. Stephen Okoronkwo joined the teaching staff much later. The school property of fifteen acres was leased from Chief Thomas Ebere for a sum of thirty dollars per year, plus gifts of fabric, yams, cola nuts, stock fish, and pineapples.

During the civil war, Brother Stephen Okoronkwo, Josiah Akandu, and Friday, the school/hospital driver, and I paid the annual land-lease rental fees to Chief Ebere.

Figure 14
Josiah Akandu and family, 1957

The school opened with the first forty-three students in 1957, opening a wider spectrum of opportunities for church expansion in Igboland and in areas where churches mushroomed in Abakaliki, Owerri, Onitcha, Aba, Rivers, and Enugu.

North of the Niger

Spreading the gospel in a barren, hostile environment is never conditioned on the ingenuity of humankind or power. Cultivating friendships with the inhabitants of the North was looked on with suspicion, apprehension, and the fear that the foreigner might contaminate the Islamic religion and their cultural life. The dread of reprisal loomed constantly in visitors' minds, but the invisible hands of God led many through the ordeal of having to venture openly, at least for some time, with faith into the North, knowing the risk. Thankfully, the Roman Catholics and especially the Sudan Interior Mission (SIM), with their hospitals ministering to the needs of lepers, were a tremendous boost; their presence helped reduced tension for others to enter the Muslim towns and cities.

Northern Nigeria is quite different from the southern sections of Nigeria—culturally, socially, politically, and in their intractable Islamic religiosity. The few Christian groups that entered the North did so with great trepidation for their lives. Those who strictly adhered to Islamic doctrine and practices viewed the presence of Christians as pollutants, corrupters of the sanctity of the minds of their people. They saw extermination of the infidels as the only solution for them to maintain the purity of their religion and culture. Any form of Western education, to them, was a viral evil and morally bankrupt.

Kaduna, as the cultural, social, and political heritage with strong allegiance to Islamism, became the catalyst for penetration into other parts of the North. Knowing the sway that Kaduna held on all Muslims, church members could not rely on Kaduna as a base from which the church could radiate into other parts of the North. Nonindigents scattered and met independently in small groups, teaching and worshipping, often in secret, in different members' homes.

But Kaduna, like Kano, was the stronghold of Islam that provided political activism and sanctuary to the radical elements of the North. As the state capital, it was situated on the Ladima River, a trade center bridging the northern states and Southern Nigeria. It was founded by the British in 1913 as the capital of the northern states. The inhabitants are *Jama'atu Sunmna Lidda'awati Wal-Jihad,* a name that, in Hausa, means Boko Haram.

Kaduna is also the city in which Islamic terrorism was hatched, with their havoc perpetuated against Christians. The city segregates Southern Nigerian citizens, isolating and confining them in the squalor, where they settle or take refuge at the fringes of the southern borders of the city. Southerners are characterized as heathens and sinners and as being unclean. Under this system, proselytizing is a dangerous endeavor, as Islamic militancy against Christian groups, particularly since 2001, more often created an unsavory relationship between the North and South.

They agitated for the implementation of Sharia law for the governance of Nigeria or Northern Nigeria, regardless. Their influence and violent militant practices have been seen on numerous occasions in violent outbreaks, destruction, and killing of Christians in the North.

Kaduna has been one of the major cities of Islamic activism in the North. It is the successor to what was known as the old Northern Nigeria. It is populated by Hausa, Gbagyi, Adara-Ham, Atyap, Bajjuu, Ninkyabo, Kurams, Karo, Zango Kutaf, and other extractions that incubate Islamic militancy. Kaduna is important because it is centrally situated and as a major trade center founded in 1813. Manoatus Nasol Islam is based here; it segregates Northern inhabitants from Southern Nigerian citizens who live in the squalor and fringes of the city.

Kaduna is also an important industrial and commercial center in Northern Nigeria. It has many colleges and universities, where one might think that Islamic victimization, intimidation, and killing of other religious group members would abate or cease. Their religion is strictly Mohammedanism in nature, which is virulently averse to any incursion of other religious groups that attempt to proselytize. It has been the seat of religious unrest and tension between Muslims and Christians; it is the city where Umar Farouk Abdulmutallab, a suspected terrorist, attempted to detonate explosives while on Northwest Airlines Flight 253 in December 2009.

The constant and often unprovoked revolt of Islamic Muslims should serve as a warning to individuals trying to pitch a Christian outpost in the area. Working in the North, one should remember a saying in Oron: *When dining with a shrewd or cunning person, use a long spoon*. And

Jesus said that Christians, while serving, should be as shrewd as a serpent and as clever as a fox (Matthew 10:16)[64] Unfortunately, the constitution of the Federation of Nigeria that promulgates freedom of speech and religion is impotent and incapable of protecting non-Muslims or enforcing its laws of freedom of speech. Maybe, in time, it will.

It is with this background that those who set out to introduce Christianity or convert the Muslims faced the danger of being persecuted or killed. Fortunately, government businesses and private concerns were in operation, transferring workers from diverse ethnic origins to the North. Individuals also sought jobs and established private businesses in the North, and among these groups were members of the church who had immigrated northward. The immigrants were, at first, only able to establish contact with those of a similar cultural background and who spoke the same dialect. Though their numbers were small, they were unique in that they carried a sense of purpose, responsibility, and devotion to Christ by spreading and establishing churches wherever they went. This sense of commitment to the glorious message was common, not only in the North but in every section of Nigeria where Christians settled in cities without the church. This act was reflective of their faith in Christ, demonstrating the sound teaching they received from the congregation with which they had worshipped before moving to new territories.

Kaduna Bible School

Figure 15
Kaduna Bible Training School

In Kaduna, as in other northern cities, indigents from the South met for socialization, though secretly at first, and those with firm conviction for the church decided to initiate house churches, consisting of the reading of the scriptures, prayers, and small biblical discussions. When members identified other members of the church, they changed the theme of their gatherings to an evangelistic religious focus. A number of these small house churches reached out to younger generations of Muslim friends, who began to study with them. As they grew larger in number, the need for a long-term, concentrated study of the scriptures arose.

On August 12, 1985, preliminary contacts were made, as Brother Etim Asuquo, of Lawanson Church in Lagos, asked Lawanson to permit him to spearhead and supervise a short-term Bible program at Kaduna. The leadership at Lawanson Church graciously approved Brother Etim Asuquo's undertaking the training at Kaduna. A few weeks thereafter, Etim left for Kaduna on a preliminary investigation. He rented a small room, which became his temporary residence, with a classroom section.

On August 12, 1985, the leaders of the church in Kaduna, aware of the danger of exposing themselves in a Muslim state but disregarding the potential threat, "used local papers to advertise, directing interested students to different locations to collect enrollment forms at Akpakpan location." Etim Asuquo said, "Members, mostly sojourners from other Nigerian states formed the nucleus of the church; but it was strange and encouraging to know that they found a church that existed in Kaduna municipality for ten years."[65]

Brother Etim Asuquo was also deeply involved with the supervision of the World Bible Course (WBC) that was gaining widespread acceptance. World Bible students were encouraged to either start a home church or learn where Christians met in their communities. Etim wrote that WBC "people here and there, are still, like in Brother C. A. O. Essien's time, taking the Bible correspondence course; they can also establish the Lord's church in their homes."

While visiting Kaduna on a sponsored survey trip, Etim wrote, "I will return to Lagos, prepare, and proceed to Kaduna in August 1985. I feel we should start the teaching program in October."[66] Etim then recommended Brother Marshall T. Ekaette, who was then serving at Oyubia, Oron, as a partner and teacher in the contemplated short-term school.

With issues afoot, Brothers E. E. Agiriga and Etim Asuquo of Lawanson Church were futuristic in their assessment of the work, saying, "With the teaching Centre in Abakpa, compared to the vast Municipality of Kaduna, it is like a drop of water in the ocean." They sought to create a "second teaching center, if not for now, but for the future while we are working very relentlessly with Brother Marshall T. Ekaette, who helped pray that we may succeed in this area."[67]

While still engrossed with the success of the program—its stability and spread to other localities of the city—they wanted to use available funds to pay rent, but they did not know for how many months. They also wanted to provide benches and other things. Still thinking ahead and to the continuity of the work, they wrote, "Since the program is going to be continuous even if we are gone, Brother Ekaette can continue and be assisted with manpower and financial resources from time to time."[68] Through Avalon Church of Christ in Los Angeles, California, many Christian friends sent one hundred dollars to subsidize the cost of transportation and a small living allowance.

The first class consisted of twenty-nine students; nineteen were Christians, and ten were non-Christians. Then Brother Etim Asuquo added, "Since we are out to help the public, Christians as the focus, workers of different faiths, we have extended the courses to Saturdays to allow workers to attend. We have few students in the morning sessions and usually more students in the evening."[69] The courses taught were New Testament and Old Testament Survey, Books of Acts, "Why I Am a Member of the Church," Denominational Doctrines, and Hermeneutics. Also, six students from the Chad Republic, the northeastern neighboring republic have been worshiping with us regularly. One of them obeyed Christ. We thank God that you [Avalon Church of Christ in Los Angeles, California] have made it possible for us to establish this program. We are also thankful that you have made it possible that Bro. Eno Otoyo and his wife, LaVera, brought the study materials for the school.[70]

The next stage of the work was to find a permanent space or building for the church to function without harassment. The leaders of the Army Elementary School permitted us to use their classroom temporarily. Meanwhile, after much searching, the leading brethren, including Brother Ekaette, negotiated for a small, affordable property for the construction of a small building that could accommodate approximately twenty-five people. Avalon Church in Los Angeles, under the leadership of Brothers Virgil Walton, Neylon Cofield, Jesse Hamilton, and William T. Milligan, raised the funds needed for the construction of the building. For about three years, the church could say they had a building where they could worship, unmolested.

Unfortunately, this did not last more than three years before a wave of Islamic militant agitators staged a revolt that resulted in the demolition of the small building, as well as other Christian groups' facilities in the area. But the threat could not stop the fearlessness, zeal, and determination of the members. This was the first congregation that had women leaders, one of whom was responsible for supervising and purchasing their building materials.

The church continued to make visible advances that reached beyond Kaduna. Brother O. A. Umoh commuted regularly between Abuja and Kaduna, which is approximately eighty kilometers. In his letter of July 3, 1985. Brother Umoh stressed the need to secure property at Abuja, the capital city of Nigeria. Soliciting financial support from churches Brother Umoh stressed the urgency of procuring property. He felt this was the right time because the government at Abuja was granting with minimum cost property to qualified churches and businesses. Unfortunately, the church was still exceedingly small and without needed resources. Brother Umoh wrote, Karu Church meets in my house. Abuja is a new and developing city. There are no buildings that one can easily rent. Existing denominations usually would first build, expecting people to attend afterward. With us, it was difficult to have Northerners because those who might be interested would rather attend a church with an existing building than those without, a situation that affected adversely the growth of the four of our churches. None of the three congregations have light or water in their buildings, which is creating problems for them.

With fortitude and faith in God, however, they persisted to hoist the banner of the New Testament church and served as springboards for the establishment of other churches in the suburbs.

The Rivers State Movement–Port Harcourt, the Garden City

Port Harcourt, the capital city of the Rivers State before the tumultuous civil war era of 1950 to 1969, had eminent politicians and a nationally recognized soccer team that was unbeatable in the country. It was a cosmopolitan trading center that attracted different nationalities, many of whom worked in the developing crude-oil sector. Port Harcourt had a railway system that connected portions of the Eastern Region through Aba, Umuahia, to the north, the second-largest shipping seaport in the nation, with an international airport, all of which made the city unrivaled as the "Garden City" of the country. Its position attracted many Nigerians to seek jobs in this industrialized city.

Religious groups like Catholics, Methodists, Anglicans, and Lutherans, which were already established, exploited the opportunities in the religiously barren land. They established schools and hospitals as their normal bait to capture the interest and hearts of the people. It is assumed that the establishment of the Church of Christ, as Brother Benedict Ibra pointed out, cannot be unconnected with Brother Young [Onwukiabu]; I could not remember his surname. This man worked as an engineer with the Nigerian National Petroleum Company (NNPC) in Alesa.

Brother Benedict said,

> "After my conversion on July 6, 1961, our preacher, Brother Johnson Ozoemelah, started to remind young men who would volunteer to go for Bible Training School at Onicha Ngwa near Aba. I had not heard

that Church of Christ has a school where
they train their ministers, I immediately
volunteered to go."[71]

Following Brother Benedict Ibra wrote, "On October 18, 1961, Brother Jim Massey arrived [at] our home for two days preaching, but I never knew that our minister made that appointment identifying me as one of the students to attend the Bible Training School at Onicha Ngwa."[72]

At this time, Rivers Province and, later, Port Harcourt Province were made up of four divisions: (1) Brass Town, with its headquarters at Brass; (2) Ahoada, with Ahoada as the headquarters; (3) Degeman, headquartered in Degeman, and (4) Ogoni, with its headquarters at Bori.

During General Gowon's first military administration, the area was changed to Rivers State. The first church was established in 1958 or '59 at B-Dere in Ogoru, in what was known as Port Harcourt State, with J. W. Nicks, as the first pioneer missionary and principal of Onicha Ngwa Bible School, visiting on numerous occasions and establishing churches.

Brother Benedict listed chronologically the churches as they were established at Omoku in Ahoada in 1960 by Brother Johnson Nosiness Melancholy. Brother Johnson visited Lagos on a business trip, where he received the truth through his uncle Samuel Okobo, who was already a member of the church at Ajegunle, Forty-Eighth Orodo

Street, in Apapa, Lagos. Benedict mentioned that Brother D. D. Isonguyo was currently the minister of the church at Ajekunle, where Leslie Diestelkamp also visited with them. The next church was planted by Brother Johnson at Omioku. Subsequently, Brother Ozoemeloah succeeded in establishing more churches at Okposi, Obigwe, Aligwu, with his two sons, one of whom, A. O. Ozowemah, preached at the University of Science and Technology, Port Harcourt, Omoku.

The church at Ubima was situated fifty kilometers north of Port Harcourt, the hometown of former governor Rotimi Amechi. The church was established in 1962 by students from Onicha Ngwa Bible School, under the leadership of Brother Moses Ibeje, once a chaplain at the Nigerian Christian Hospital. This church witnessed many difficulties because of the ostensible presence of denominations that harassed them, but they refused to surrender, persevering over the years to acquire one of the best church buildings in the state.[73]

Ezekiel Etche's congregation is about forty kilometers north of Port Harcourt. It was planted by Brother Benjamin Ihenacho, a student of Onicha Ngwa Bible School in 1960 or 1961. If one preaches in this congregation, someone in the congregation said, he will not be rich. (Of course, we do not preach for money or seek riches.) But one important fact or characteristic of this congregation is that "it does not like to stay without a preacher—but would make the sacrifice to have one, the last of whom was Brother Azu Chika, who is currently preaching in one of the congregations at Enugu."[74]

The church continued to spread to other areas of the state, often encountering the opposition and displeasure of denominations. The church at Nchia, Eleme, was established by another student of Onicha Ngwa Bible School in 1964. The church suffered a singular setback due to the inordinate desire of individuals who were seeking jobs that they assumed the white men could offer them. Most of the job seekers—church members and a few from the public—were disappointed, while the small churches persisted and have survived the onslaught of unbelievers (Satan). For example, during the civil war, many churches could not meet because of (1) members' fear of being conscripted into the army, (2) young ladies' fear of being raped by lawless soldiers, (3) those in urban areas returning to their villages without jobs, and (4) others running into the bushes for safety, a common trend in all the sectors of the war.

Progressively, the church continued to gain momentum. [The late] "Abraham Udeme established the church in his home village, Okarki, Engenni, in the then Ahoada Division. James Momah, of blessed memory, also established a church at Okpoma in the then Brass Division, at Obonnema in Degema Division and one late Yelloowe Oreke planted a church at Akabuka, also in former Ahoada Division."[75]

The dreadful nature of the civil war forced many to flee their homes and forced churches to disperse to numerous safe centers, where a smattering of people congregated. The havoc wrought by the war left wounds; though healed by time, the indelible scars remain. Brother Benedict wrote that the effects of the civil war were numerous; "When we returned to our village, we hadn't any means for survival, no money except, when we heard that Brother Stephen Okoronkwo had returned from the US bringing relief materials and money to be distributed among churches, "I personally went to Aba to meet him where upon he gave me ten pounds each for seven churches, and this amount was shared congregationally no matter the numerical size of the congregation. From Aba I went to Oron where Brother Otoyo and his wife gave us five sterling pounds as a portion of relief money sent through Brother Wendell Kee in Cameroons for the Nigerian Brethren."[76]

The brethren in the Rivers area persisted in establishing churches in many other villages. Sister Agnes Olowu was continually active in spreading the word up to Ogoloma, the capital of Balyeisa, and at Okrika. The church at Yerago was established by the Port Harcourt congregation, including the church at Andoni, which was sponsored by the students at the Bible Training School at Asarama. This school became defunct because of a lack of financial resources. Brother Douglas Lawyer and

Douglas Wheeler used to visit to encourage the brethren in these areas.

Like a steamboat, the preachers and members kept rolling, pushing, persuading, converting, and establishing more churches in other localities. The story of the growth of churches in the Rivers State continued to attract many unbelievers, which emphasized the difference in a way that was opposed to the established denominational doctrines. Villagers felt the impact of the movement, and those who could reason or conceptualize the teachings of the New Testament readily welcomed and embraced the truth.

Figure 16

Ikot Ekpene Church, first group of members, 1965

Ikot Ekpene, the political and cultural capital of Annang and popularly known as the Raffia City, is a densely populated town in the present Akwa Ibom State. From Ikot Ekpene, it is twenty miles to Uyo, the state capital. Traveling twenty-four miles westward from Ikot Ekpene, the Nigerian Christian Hospital is observed on the highway to Aba, a major commercial city that competes with the Onitcha market. On the border of the Ngwa and Annang tribes is a stream that separates the two warring tribes, which have had skirmishes, making coexistence on the border complicated and unbearable.

For example, even with the presence of the Nigerian Christian Bible School, which existed for over twenty years, the deep-seated animosity flared up, with agitators pillaging and destroying the school property and, in 1969, massacring a few people, including Titi, the deaf sister of our beloved Brother Stephen Okoronkwo. The horrific and dastardly event understandably forced Brother Stephen to evacuate the Onicha Ngwa Bible School compound, a place he had served and had grown to love. This was also why a garrison of soldiers was stationed on the hill toward Ikot Ekpene for more than fifty years to protect the people. Often, however, the safety of the people did not happen because the soldiers and police never knew when or where a situation might explode. The soldiers were ineffective because they too were afraid for their lives.

The British troops that arrived the area in about 1903 marched and settled at Ikot Ekpene, where a garrison of soldiers was stationed at Uyo, through Abak to what was then Opobo, now Ikot Abasi. These movements were to protect the commercial ventures and missionaries who had settled in these areas, where several of the dominant denominations had already established themselves and had the protection of the soldiers. In the early 1950s, the Church of Christ first arrived, scrambling to have a foothold in the area.

Brother Udo Akpan Ukpong Mba, of Nto Abatekpe family in Ikot Ekpene, provided a comprehensive narration of the beginning of the church in the Ikot Ekpene communities. He was converted on September 22, 1952, by Brother J. U. Akpan from Ibiaku Ikot Oku, Ibiono. He wrote:

> "The church was established through the effort of Late Brother E. U. Essien (Alias) Etok Udut Ukpong Essien and three other members namely, U. A. Ukpong, Okposi Etok Udut, and Sister Agnes Etok Udut, four of them received bible instructions from Brother E. U. Essien, and the first place of worship was in the home of late Brother E. U. Essien at Mbot, 30 Spring Road, Ikot Ekpene on December 28, 1952. Many who heard of the church started mockingly calling the church after

Brother Etok Udut, because the church met in his house. To avoid the linkage and derision, we packed to Nto Ebiekwa family Hall."[77]

Six new converts were made, and soon the congregation grew to ten members. The church was young, and members had extremely limited financial resources. Brother J. U. Udoh "singlehandedly supported minister Uyo Aban who within a short time left the congregation because the support was inadequate."[78] Brother J. U. Akpan then decided to minister to the church every first day of the week. "On a Sunday, two strangers, Brother Edet Essien, from Ediene Ikot Obio Imo, and Nelson Dan Isonguyo, both students of Ikot Osurua Teachers Training College (TTC), visited to worship with us. They suggested, instead of meeting in a member's house, they should get permission to meet in a nearby primary school. We met with the headmaster of the school, who granted us permission to worship at the Universal Primary Education School."[79]

Brother J. U. Akpan also helped to recruit Brother Fearless Akpan of Ukat Aran, a student of the Bible Training School at Ukpom Abak, to minister to them. Soon, the church suffered reverses, with members dwindling from ten to the original four. A quit notice to vacate the house where they worshipped was issued to them. Later, Brother Peter Akpan Eka and his three children, along with Akpan Offong, were converted, thereby increasing the membership to nine. Without a meeting place, the neophyte member said, "Offong asked us to move to his house, which we did."[80]

But before long, a theological argument erupted, in which Offong vindictively seized their church property and made them pay him before he would release it. Again, they moved, this time through the urging of Mr. Abak Ada, who gave them a place near the central post to settle. Their accommodation problem, however, was not over. To their dismay, after investing in the purchase and construction of a building, for which Brother Wendell Broom helped through matching fund finances, they were forced again to move. Later, they discovered that the property issued to them did not belong to Mr. Akpan Enang. Amid these turbulent experiences, their faith was unshaken, and they did not relent in the reclamation of the lost and the planting of churches in the neighboring villages.

In 1963, after having wandered from site to site, Brother Peter Akpan Eka suggested "the brethren should move to Ikot Ekpene Town. We then went and hired the United African Company (UAC) warehouse."[81] In 1965, they purchased a piece of land owned by two brothers, Ukpong Mba and Udo Akpan Ukpong Mba, for the sum of 150 pounds. Brother Udo Akpan Mba wrote in the church history document that "Brother Eno Otoyo loaned us one hundred pounds without any interest while we raised fifty pounds to construct a mud building, and at that time, our preacher was Brother Ita Bassey Udo Orun from Idoro with Brother Essien Ekanem helping from time to time."[82]

The civil war forced many of our members to scatter to different parts of the state as refugees. On January 18, 1970, Brother Udo Akpan Ukpong Mba wrote, "I came back with my wife to meet Brother Peter Akpan Eka from Itu, and Sunday Umo Eka from Nkwot Ikot Umo who joined us to worship at Ukpong Udoka's compound along Ikot Udo Offiong Road."[83]

Not having much of a choice, they returned to worship at the Universal Primary Education. N. R. Umana, from Manta, Abak, unfortunately, left without notice, but Dr. Sunday Peter Ekanem "went to Ukpom to plead that Brother Otoyo send us another preacher.[84]"

N. J. Eka Iko, from Obong Ntak, was sent in 1972. He was a man with an unusual ability to endure and believed he served the living God, and, in the struggle, he and others established the following ten churches, some in Ikot Ekpene Township, others in the periphery of the town. Brother E. J. Udofia was selected to serve the Abak Road congregation for over twenty years.

Ibiakpan	Ukana Ikot Ide
Ikpe Ikot Akpan	Abak Oko
Nsit Ikpe	Itak/Abiaokpo
Ikot Abia Idem	Ikot Abias Eyop
Imama Nto Eton	Ukana Ikot Ntuen

Makurdi

Makurdi is the capital of Benue State. It was established in the early 1920s as a port on the Benue River, where the early European explorers established commercial companies, like the United African Company (UAC) and John Holt, as major business enterprises that catered to the welfare of Europeans. The railway bridge, built in 1932, made Makurdi a vital link and commercial crossroad between the northeastern and eastern states of Nigeria.

Makurdi is an important city, with many educational establishments, such as the Federal University of Agriculture, the Nigerian Army, and the School of Military Engineering, headquarters of the Twenty-Second Battalion for Nigeria. Numerous state and federal institutions, like the railway system, have made Makurdi a relatively calm city, without the presence or influence of Islamic militant extremism. The major northern route is the Makurdi-Lafia Jos Road, and the southern roads link Makurdi-Otokpo-Enugu and the Makurdi-Yander-Adikpu to Calabar in Cross River. These roads enhanced transportation and provided easy access for communication in the state.

The Roman Catholics first settled there in the fifteenth century, through the work of Saint Augustine and Capuchin monks from Portugal. They settled briefly and then withdrew after two years. The vacuum was filled by several commercial entities in collaboration with the Anglican Church, the purpose of which was to expand trade and evangelization, respectively. Before the advent of the Church of Christ in the area, government establishments, such as the railway system, colleges, and schools, including the Anglican Church and, later, the Roman Catholics, made many cities in Benue State, particularly Makurdi, less prevalent to hostile Islamic encroachment.

Before 1987, when Brother Sunday Unogwo Onah was converted through an intensive biblical study from the World Bible program, other individuals were enrolled in similar Bible studies. The groundwork was laid for future expansion and development of churches in the three major areas of Benue State, Tiv, Jukeen, and part of Tiv; another section is Etelus and Benue East, comprising Idomas and Igedes.

Brother Sunday Unogwu Onah hailed from Ijigban, Benue, and was a Hamilton member—a special group within the legislature—of the Benue State Legislature in 1992. He was converted in 1987 through Bible correspondence study.

CHAPTER 5

Afro-Americans Join the Fray

Francis & Wilma Carson

Figure 17

For more than twelve years, the pioneering work of the church in Nigeria was conducted by the Caucasian missionaries, who were the catalysts to the movement. The Caucasian brethren carried the burden of financially supporting the work; training the greatest caliber of workers, some of whom were incredibly young but zealous and eager to undertake the teaching and preaching; and organizing the scripturally managed systems that changed significantly the spiritual and educational topography of the Churches of Christ missions in Nigeria.

The Afro–American churches were struggling for self-identity. There was political turmoil, the human rights movement, and economic disparity that hovered around black citizens. Issues, such as their being perennially labeled as slaves, were emotionally damaging. The Afro-American actions were controlled and regarded as less than human. In W. W. Morrison's book, *The Shaping of a Brotherhood*, he wrote, "You were affected by segregation from birth to death. You could not sit at the same lunch counter with white, could not drink from the same water fountain, could not use the same rest room. Riding in the front of the bus was prohibited."[85]

Ben Harris and Janice Bryant, in *Martin Luther King Jr: The Enduring Legacy of the American Dream*, noted that before the black citizens of Alabama could vote, they were required to pass an intentionally confusing literacy test, pay a punitive poll tax, and secure the endorsement of a white voter. There were segregated and demoralizing signs that excluded or designated black citizens to use inferior amenities. Signs, such as "Colored Waiting Room" or "Private Property: No Parking, Driving Through, or Turning Around were conspicuously posted."[86]

Systemic racism and economic conditions made it impossible for black persons to advance. They were paid less than whites to do the same job with the same experience and credentials. Schools were segregated, without equality in the type of building structures. They were restricted to indecent facilities that failed to inspire and encourage a healthy educational environment. They received the dilapidated hand-me-down books and inferior study materials, if available.[87] Black teachers were inadequately paid, and, in one situation in the 1960s, a white administrator's office was modernly furnished and had adequate heating, but the black dean of students was always shivering in his poorly furnished office, without an adequate heating system.

These contentious issues affected the Afro-Americans' ability to think positively, globally, as they knew of the disproportionate ills and means for any social, political, or economic advancement. Their wings were clipped, and they could not consider any mission beyond their personal and local needs, which were hardly met. They could not think of getting out of their restrictive shell. A few churches, however, like Figueroa Church in Los Angeles; Avalon Church, Los Angeles; Ninth Street Church, Cedar Crest, Dallas, Texas; Third Ward Church, Houston; and South Union Church, Houston, Texas, provided sanctuary for a few Nigerian Christians. The University Church of Christ in Cleveland, Ohio, where Levi Kennedy ministered, actively shared their love and their meager means but hesitated in venturing into a long-term mission relationship or adventure that might sap their inadequate and limited resources.

It took years of encouragement and planning for them to think of any mission work. In 1956, Brother Dr. Nnana Ibokette Isonguyo; Essien Akpan Essien, MD; and I met Brother Francis F. Carson at Pepperdine University. Both Essien Akpan Essien and I, however, met F. F. Carson and Levi Kennedy at the Southwestern Christian College campus during Southwestern's annual lectureship in 1957. In time, Carson and Kennedy became the first two Afro-American brethren who showed genuine interest in visiting Nigeria on a mission.

When F. F. Carson visited Richard N. Hogan at the Figueroa Church in Los Angeles, he was ministering at the Southside Church of Christ in Richmond, California. Levi Kennedy was one of the most distinguished and recognized preachers in the history of the Afro-American church's movement and was a contemporary of Richard Nathaniel Hogan, John Steven Winston, George Edmond Steward, and Francis F. Carson. Kennedy was one of the cofounders of Southwestern Christian College, Terrell, Texas. On May 21, 1931, "trusting in the Lord," Kennedy left his lucrative coal- and ice-truck business for a preaching job that paid a meager five dollars a week.

A host of such men preached and were not paid—or "occasionally were paid with a chicken or two, a dozen eggs, and perhaps a sack of sweet potatoes.'[88] When someone asked Levi Kennedy how he "made it with such meager resource, Kennedy's response was, 'I didn't make it; the Lord made it for me."[89] He accompanied F. F. Carson on the Nigerian mission trip, and they were an invaluable, inseparable team. When they traveled to one of the congregations that was converted en masse, Carson observed some musical instruments—drums, a tambourine, a flute. Without hesitation, he asked the leaders to remove the instruments, as they were not an acceptable means for worship, nor was there a teaching that approved the use of such a method in worship in the New Testament. To accommodate the request, the new members in the church quietly (to hospitably acquiesce) moved the instruments to the back of the building.

Significantly, F. F. Carson was the first person, with his congregation of Afro-American extraction, that sponsored a Caucasian minister, Brother Tom Trone, on a foreign mission. This gesture served as a prelude to Carson's dream of entering a foreign field—Nigeria. Six months later, I joined Essien Akpan Essien at Pepperdine, and we both became instrumental in persuading F. F. Carson to consider a trip to Nigeria. Fortunately, Carson did not need much persuasion; he was an activist and was passionate about Africa. He indicated he had always wanted to visit the fatherland and would be ready to travel to Nigeria when he could assemble a group to travel with him.

In 1958, I had a conference with Carson in the Christian Echo Printing Press office, where a discussion arose that included Brother Richard N. Hogan, the minister at Figueroa Church of Christ. Carson tried to persuade Hogan to travel with him to Nigeria, but Hogan declined, due to his intense, phobic aversion to flying. Hogan quipped, "If I could drive on water, I would be glad to go."[90]

Soon after this, Carson contacted Brother Levi Kennedy, who consented to go, and he made a great companion for the missionary adventure.

Ukpekpe and the First Negro Church of Christ

The entrance of T. J. O. Ukpekpe into the religious scene of the Church of Christ sparked some interest and controversy. Ukpekpe became the founder of the First Negro Church of Christ in his village, Utu Etim Ekpo. Somehow, he established and maintained ongoing contact with Brother F. F. Carson through Dr. Ibokette and Essien Akpan Essien, who encouraged Carson to make a trip to Nigeria. Strangely, Ukpekpe got wind of this and contacted Carson about visiting

Nigeria because he had many members waiting to be converted.

On November 6, 1961, Ukpekpe wrote to Carson:

"Dear Brother in Christ,

> Greetings in the name of Jesus Christ. I am happy to inform you that a greater number of the people in this area and abroad have embraced the news of the First Negro Church of Christ, we are expecting when it might be for you to reach this country in person."

F. F. Carson never created the name *First Negro Church of Christ*. This was Ukpekpe's brainchild; perhaps it was Ukpekpe's conniving approach to entice Carson to visit. Continuing, Ukpekpe wrote, "I have no doubt that you have taken the name of Mr. I. Akpan whom I wished to be trained for this mission when you assume the management in Nigeria."[91]

Based on the trend of events, Ukpekpe positioned himself to be the clearinghouse and the absolute manager of the First Negro Church of Christ, again assuring Carson, "I have secured the building with sufficient rooms which will accommodate you and your team."[92] To impress Brother Carson further, he wrote, "We are living in a township and we have pipe borne water." Utu Etim Ekpo, where Ukpekpe lived, did not have pipe-borne water, nor was it a township, unless, perhaps, he meant Abak or Uyo, two towns a distance away from Utu Etim Ekpo. He then recommended, "If it were possible, I would impress upon you to include the building of a hospital as one of your projects. I am an old man *[indeed, he was at this stage]* and would remind you to put the question of transport into your heart when you come over here."[93]

Ukpekpe was not pretentious in exposing his motive. Attempting to lure F. F. Carson and Kennedy, he played the race card and spread seeds of discord against the successful and vibrant ongoing work done by the Caucasian brethren. Ukpekpe wrote, "Most of the churches of Christ in Nigeria managed by American Caucasian had died, and some woke up [were revived] during your stay with us." This was a blatant negation of the truth. The reason, he opined, was "bad management and negligence of duty." In the same letter of November 6, 1962, Ukpekpe asked for "paying salaries for preachers, transportation, building, a full-fledged hospital, [and the awarding of] university scholarships."[94]

He also advocated separation from the existing, thriving mission, desiring his to be "independent of theirs." Ukpekpe, not yet grounded in the scriptures was, in effect, seeking material rewards that, he hoped, might be dispensed by the First Negro Church of Christ missionaries. Not surprising, a few fortune-seeker preachers, who were trained at the Church of Christ premier theological school, aligned themselves with Ukpekpe, hoping that money would be poured into their personal coffers. Men like Walter Umoh, of Ikot Nya in Western Nsit, and Jeremiah U. E. Ekpo, of Abak, who got Carson's address from his uncle Amos Udoakang, aligned themselves with Ukpekpe.

The needs expressed in Ukpekpe's letter, though many and varied, were legitimate in that the Church of Christ had only one secondary school at Ukpom. They had no hospital, except the Nigerian Christian Hospital at Aba. Preachers did not have adequate financial support and had to rely on the pittance from village congregations. However, Ukpekpe's concern and motive were directed toward acquisition of transportation and a leadership role, which were obvious and suspect. The attempt also to interject a bridge that would cause disaffection between the white group that had existed for thirty-seven years and the dream of the First Negro Church of Christ, the new child on the block, by playing the race card appeared disingenuous.

Brother David Anako, in his attempt to please both sides, wrote to Ukpekpe on November 6, 1962:

> "Brother Carson, if I tell you anything
> about our brethren over here, I believe
> that you know it will be between you

> and me. I believe that God's time is the best, I know you will find favor before the Nigerian people more than the white brethren."[95]

The preceding statement, coming from the source in his own writing and as a dear and diligent worker, appeared cunning, insidious, and mischievous.

A welcome address, presented to F. F. Carson and Levi Kennedy by the chiefs, elders, and counselors at Ediene and on behalf of the people of the Ediene Abak clan, stated, "We also call your attention to the fact that we do not believe that to Anglicize [that is, to change] the name of the Church of Christ will be proper. We would therefore wish the Negro Church of Christ be changed forthwith."[96]

Fortunately, both Carson and Kennedy were aware of the import of such underhanded machinations by Mr. Ukpekpe and did not fall into this trap. On January 23, 1965, Carson wrote,

> "What we [the church in Richmond] plan to do in Nigeria is not in any way, shape, form or fashion in opposition to what the brethren are doing there already. If it is not clear to the Nigerian brethren [Ukpekpe's group] at present, I give my word, it will be clear to them in time."

This meant the First Negro Church of Christ—as well as the agitation for the leadership of the group and/ or whatever any person wanted to gain materially—was dead. As members of the Church of Christ, we must present unity and a cooperative stance as a unit of believers before the public but not only publicly. In the first century and for centuries to follow, the name fostered unity of the believers and gave "us" the "rule of faith," as was enunciated in the Apostles' Creed, as well as the New Testament.

After consultation with Kennedy, Carson, as a gesture of concern and to not abandon Ukpekpe, who had led over a thousand people to be converted and was instrumental in pushing for Carson's visit, agreed to fulfill a promise by initiating short-term three-month biblical training near Ukpekpe. The teachers were J. U. Ekong, T. J. Akpan, Matthew George, James Eshiet, and Effiong A. Enyenihi. This also included Brother David Anako and I, as the supervisors. Ukpekpe was made the caretaker. In Brother David Anako's letter of November 5, 1962, he noted that the curriculum included the following courses:

- Bible Topics
- Acts of the Apostles.
- Old Testament Survey
- Harmony of the Gospels

- Epistles
- General Epistles
- Preparation and Delivery of Sermon
- New Testament Church

After numerous deliberations in 1965, Brother Levi Kennedy sent $160, saying, "That should take care of our January commitment to the 16 preachers."[97] Brother David Anako was closely involved with the three-month training, which helped stabilize the faith of over one thousand members of the churches brought by Ukpekpe. The effects of group conversion were that people had a "mass mind," in which only the leader generated thoughts, and the people simply accepted, unquestionably, decisions made from the top. The different Bible classes were to dispel such a mindset, while supplanting the biblical organizational structure. On December 11, 1962, Brother Anako wrote to inform Brother Carson, "We have had a phenomenally successful meeting on the 10th with the preachers. Forty-five showed up as candidates for the three-month study. Six field evangelists have been appointed for various centers to continue preaching and teaching."[98]

Some of the students who were not fluent in the English language were taught in Efik. Brother N. R. Umana, who was one of the facilitators in the First

Negro Church of Christ movement, was lukewarm—if not disenchanted, aggrieved, and concerned—about the consequences of the Nigerian Civil War. Brother Carson, in communicating on December 28, 1969, to Umana, opined, "We also believe in God's plan that Nigeria overcomes the temptation despite the uncounted losses in human lives, life stocks, houses and homes, and money, etc."[99] He prayed that Nigeria would remain to battle faithfully to the end.

There were torrents of solicitations to Carson on various issues. Most were for study aids and commentaries, but some requested financial assistance. The class was growing beyond the number originally contemplated. On December 12, 1962, Carson wrote, first, we anticipated a class of 30 students for three months at a cost of $600 [for six months]. Last week I received a letter from Brother Glen Martin who informed me that we had 70 students in three schools, and that it would cost at least $450 per month more than we had expected.

The three-month Bible training equipped the saints with rudimentary lessons that helped sustain the faith of the young churches. As the church grew, the needs to venture into unknown territories also grew, but workers were in short supply. One of the letters received at the time grabbed the interest of Carson, who, unfortunately, was a one-man trumpeter. The letter came, however, from two brethren from the Cameroons at the Modeka and Kongwe churches in the Mungo area of West Cameroon. The letter, dated December 10, 1962, expressed that "the two congregations were established here in 1957 through the efforts of Wendell Broom, and two evangelists were sent over to Cameroons the same year to take charge of the congregations in Kumba, Victoria, and Tiko."[100] These, then, were the first three churches outside of Nigeria in the Cameroons. Continuing, Elangwe, the leading evangelist in the Cameroons, wrote, "...these evangelists visited us from time to time and instructed us in the way of the Lord. But when their support was cut off in 1959, they had to get secular jobs to earn their livings, which made the work stagnant. Yet we continued to preach the gospel, and we were able to establish two little congregations in Yato and Missaka."[101]

The initial members of the church were foreigners, mostly from Nigeria. The only Cameroonian natives were Brother Benedict T. Kuhtsu and Damasus Elangwe, who were the first fruits of the Lord. In 1962, we were sent to the Bible Training School at Ukpom, where Brother I. E. Udoh and his wife were recommended to work with us.

Figure 18

Damasus Ngota Elangwe and family

The First Fruits of the Gospel in Cameroons

Brother Damasus Ngota Elangwe moved with his family from Cameroon to study at Ukpom. Both he and Benedict Toh Kutsu were great Christian ambassadors for the Cameroons. While still at Ukpom Bible School, Brother Elangwe's letter of October 4, 1962, painted a common and familiar theme:

"Like many other places, our country has fields quite ripe, but no laborers. We were the first two men in Cameroons to obey the gospel, and we are the only ones yet preparing for the labor in the field. West Cameroons had been visited by Brothers Wendell Broom, Eugene Peden, Glen Martin, and E. Essien; and we have seven little congregations at present in Tiko, Kumba, Modeka, Congue, Barambi Koto, Yato and Mbonge."[102]

Like C. A. O. Essien, Elangwe asked that Carson's congregation send missionaries to the Cameroons. Personnel were scarce, however, and unable to meet the growing needs of the churches in many communities. The Cameroon request, unfortunately, had to be put on the back burner temporarily. Carson could not afford the time or the financial resources to undertake the challenge in Cameroon.

The Rocking Boat—Paul and Barnabas Syndrome

The sharp but brotherly disagreement that arose between Paul and Barnabas as to whether to take John Mark on the second missionary journey forced them to go their separate ways. F. F. Carson and Levi Kennedy encountered a disagreement—though not serious—as to which group to align themselves. Kennedy opted to join camp with the already-proven mission work that the Caucasian brethren had done. Carson acknowledged the good work the Caucasian brethren had done. In his letter of September 2, 1965, he wrote, "If the house where Brother John Beckloff lived was still vacant and was serviceable to us when we arrive, I won't mind staying there, but I prefer being in Aba since I will be trying to help Dr. Henry Farrar."

Earlier, on April 15, 1964, he had expressed his intention: "My plans are to bring my wife and another sister of the church with me to set up a clinic and then a hospital somewhere."[103] Instead of joining with the white brethren, he preferred to undertake independent mission work, separate and apart from what existed. This meant that he chose to maintain contact with the Ukpekpe group, where there was a strong administrative structure and faithful Christians to supervise his efforts.

In 1971, Brother F. F. Carson was already involved with the construction of a borehole water system for the Christian Secondary Technical College, Oyubia Town, Oron. On December 8, 1971, Carson visited Brother Louis and Sister Ruby Holland, of Figueroa Church, Los Angeles, who had already visited Nigeria. In the *Nigerian Informer*, published by Southside Church of Christ in Richmond, California, Carson wrote:

> I made a trip to Los Angeles for the purpose of getting some firsthand information from him [Brother Holland] about the situations relative to the needs of the suffering in Nigeria. He said, "Brother Carson, we must help, we must do something. And I responded by saying, I am so thankful for these brothers' zeal

and determination to work on behalf of
the less fortunate."[104]

To encourage Brother Carson to do whatever he could, the following caption was published in the December issue of the *Nigerian Informer*, a monthly publication on behalf of the Nigerian mission work: "Whatever you do, don't stop with the water system!"[105]

This, then, was the prelude to Brother Carson's desire for long-term involvement in the Nigerian work and in cooperation with me; I was instrumental in referring and guiding Brother Okon Mkpong to Francis Carson. Meanwhile, Brother Emmanson, Wilson Nkanta, S. Ekpo, and others jointly wrote to Carson: "We believe that it is God's plan that Nigeria overcome the temptation" of overindulgence, greed, and tribal hatred. They further stated that with the tumultuous, senseless "loss of human lives, livestock, demolition of homes, loss of money, etc. Nigerian churches will ever remain to battle faithfully to the end and to wear the crown."[106] They also wrote that the Lord's church began at Abat Afaha Obo in 1964 with sixteen baptisms, and in a short period, the congregation had grown to seventy-nine members.

It did not take long to identify the caliber of the person for whom F. F. Carson was looking to oversee the mission program that would be managed under the direction of Southside Church of Christ in Richmond, California.

Brother (now Chief) Okon Mkpong was available, and he became the third link of the tripartite. Our illustrious Brother Mkpong, as referred by Otoyo, took over the supervision of one section of the short-term training program, which ultimately led to the establishment of one of our most successful and progressive high schools in the state, the Nigerian Christian Institute in Uyo, Akwa Ibom State.

CHAPTER 6

A Few Faithful Men

Because of the difficulty in gathering information, only a few churches and individuals are cited here. There were many, but these few reflect the desire and vigor of the men who, with self-motivation and a sense of adventure, launched into many regions and tribes in Nigeria, teaching and preaching on their own, without prior training. These men, whether recorded here or not, were instrumental in jump-starting churches. They met in individual members' houses, in school buildings, and in market centers. These were men of great determination; in many instances, courageous but were restricted for lack of a good formal education. They were also handicapped by lack of a dependable means of livelihood. They faced adversities, rebuffs, and disdain; they were ridiculed by those who viewed them as threats. All they had were worn out Bibles, except the belief in God's sovereignty through the promise of the salvation in Christ, the Savior.

One cannot help but pause in awe at the heroism of these soldiers of the cross, who persevered to champion God's kingdom on earth. The expansion of the church was due, in part, to the availability of jobs for transferred government officials, as well as private concerns that existed, and indigents recruited from other states. Members who moved into the northern states, though not equipped with a full knowledge of the teachings of the New Testament church, had the zeal, foresight, and rudimentary knowledge to teach the basic principles effectively. It therefore was not unusual for lay members to be important factors in starting the church, usually on the fringes of the cities. Many met secretly in homes, mostly in the Muslim regions, where their lives were in danger from Islamic militancy.

Though there were already numerous denominational churches in the Delta State, as in other communities, the area was barren in terms of a Church of Christ presence. In time, the areas became fertile soil for evangelization. The initial thrust was launched by two students, D. D. IsongUyo, and Solomon Etuk, who, after graduating from Ukpom Bible Training College in 1956, embarked on exploratory mission work, first in Midwestern State, where the men settled in Sapele. These ministers came from the old Eastern Region of Nigeria in 1960. After staying for a while, Brother D. D. IsongUyo moved to Lagos, where he labored and established the first church at Ajegunle. Brother IsongUyo's departure forced Brother Solomon U. U. Etuk to move to Benin City, now the capital city of Edo State. In Benin, Solomon Etuk labored to plant the "first church, which now meets at No. 1 Church Avenue, Benin City.[107]

A church was also established at Ikom in Sapele, and from there, the missionaries traveled to Ugheli in the former Western Urhobo Division of the Midwestern Region in 1965. At Ugheli, they evangelized every part of Ugheli and baptized twelve souls in one day. Another church met at the Rice Mill Street, Ugheli. There was no resident missionary except Brother David Kerume, who was the first minister to lead the Nigerian missionary to Warri, where evangelism was conducted for a short time.

Brother Edwin Ekure stated that the first Nigerian missionary met in a house at Iyara Street, Warri, with Brother Vincent, who occasionally visited with the missionaries. But the bulk of the evangelization of the area was conducted by indigents who sponsored and initiated contacts with the people. For example, Brother Ezekiel Emetefeh met at the primary school with six initial members, which constituted the Grey Street Church at Uvivie, Delta. Later, Paul Mbaba was responsible for the establishment of the church at MM3 on Kakpa Road, Effurum, where they worshipped at the Briglite Tomorrow School. Brother Mark Eneme reported that they worshipped at Jugbale Market, but then Brother Paul E. Ekpo, a native of Akwa Ibom State, who migrated into the area, was their minister. Brother Eneme also reported that Orchuwhevu was one of the congregations in Udu Local Government Area.

At Oshimih Local Government Area, Brother Abraham Micharu was the first preacher, and Brother Ralph Perry, a US missionary, was of major encouragement in the establishment of the church at Opete, which met at the Opete Town Hall, Ovwoan, Udu. It is reported that Brother Good Luck Omojevwe was one of the leading members at Udu Road Church, established in Udu LGA. Brother Good Luck's presence enhanced the growth of the church in many communities.

Jacob A. Achinefu

Brother Jacob Achinefu was born on May 5, 1942, in Amaoji, Amano Ngwa. His parents were members of the Anglican Church, so as a child, he naturally also became a member. Brother Achinefu ascribes his contact with the Church of Christ through Brother Rees Bryant, who was instrumental in converting him during a debate between a Seventh-day Adventist church pastor and Bryant in 1955. Impressed with the debate topics and the way Bryant responded to many biblical questions, he made up his mind to become a member of the Church of Christ. His demonstrated keen interest in studying the Bible resulted in his accepting the offer to study at the Onicha Ngwa Bible College (1959–62). While teaching at the Bible

College, he preached full time for a short period, until his admission into Lubbock [Texas] Christian College (University), where he earned a bachelor's degree; later, he enrolled at the University of Texas for a master's degree in English.

Brother Achinefu was dedicated to the cause and zealous in declaring the intent and purposes of the church in many of the communities where he established churches. His excellent teaching ability and knowledge of the scriptures contributed to his being employed to teach at Onicha Ngwa Bible College, his alma mater.

Essien Ekanem

Brother Essien Ekanem was mighty in the scriptures and was a colleague and contemporary of Brother C. A. O. Essien. At the initial stages of the development of the church, both he and Essien were close collaborators in planning strategies for launching evangelistic missions in many villages. Brother Ekanem's ancestry is from Ntan Ekere, a village a few miles from Ikot Usen, where the church started. He was an independent thinker, and as a student of the scriptures, he sought proof of every teaching and every religious practice, especially when he encountered opposition from the denominational teachers. He was diligent and assiduous in the study of the scriptures from many Bible correspondence courses, which, with regular practice, qualified him as an apologetic.

My impression upon traveling and working with him was that Brother Ekanem was a very humble man, sympathetic and compassionate in his dealings with people, and always willing to share and to take the time to listen to people. When meeting and talking with him, one would come away feeling that he was indeed a devoted, honest man. His seemingly meek demeanor could be misinterpreted as a sign of weakness, but Ekanem was never a pushover; he was resolute and ready to stand his ground. He spent his energy and knowledge initially in Ibiono. Later, his attention was diverted to converting and establishing churches in Akpabuyo communities and in Okoyong of the Cross River State. He traveled to the west, including Midwest, heralding the good news about Christ and his church.

Songbooks were published primarily by denominational churches, and there often were not enough to meet the needs of churches. The Church of Christ was young and without Christian patriots or churches that could invest in the publication of songbooks. It was not long before Ekanem saw that the need for songbooks could be circulated among Churches of Christ members. For months, he undertook the tedious task of translating songs from English into Efik, which eventually were compiled and published as the *Songs of the Church*. He also published tracts for preachers to use and circulate during their evangelistic campaigns.

Brother Essien Ekanem was a protégée of Brother C. A. O. Essien, and they were inseparable strategists in determining where to launch their evangelistic outreach. Ekanem attended several Bible training classes taught by C. A. O. Essien; as Essien's right-hand man, Ekanem also taught many of these classes and was an esteemed confidant, prior to the appearance of Diestelkamp on the scene. Brother Ekanem became one of the proponents of the anti-movement. This was a separatist group of Church of Christ members that opposed churches' support of orphan homes, education through church funds, or benevolence or missionary work through an intermediary, which brother Ekanem learned from Diestelkamp. Their theological position and teaching were that churches were not commanded by the scriptures to conduct or to be actively involved in providing funds from the church treasury to support benevolence to nonmembers or to establishing and maintaining secular institutions, such as schools, hospitals, or other such institutions, through the church.

Did they forget (or not read) Paul's injunction in Galatians? "Let us not become weary in doing good for at the proper time we will reap a harvest if we do not give up. Therefore, as we have opportunity, let us do good to all people, especially to those who belong to the family of believer."[108]

Upon learning Brother Ekanem's views and position, Effiong John Ebong, swung to the negative side of the pendulum, which eventually led to the split within the church.

What logical or justifiable explanation could one give for Brother Ekanem or Brother Effiong John Ebong, the two protagonists (prima donnas) of the anti-movement, to jump ship? By no means were these men fickle-minded. Brother Ekanem's separation came soon after the arrival of Diestelkamp, who indoctrinated him (Ekanem) on the anti-movement views and teachings. The anti-movement contend that church support to and financing the cost of establishing and maintaining educational institution is unscriptural and sinful. They also belief and teach, it is wrong for a church to send money through a second party-a legally and scripturally constituted church, to handle support designated for a preacher. The establishment and support of benevolence through institutions like orphan homes, schools are contrary to biblical doctrine for them. It was difficult to know whether Ekanem's and Effiong J. Ebong's departure or objection was due to their not receiving their stipend directly, rather than depending on Brother C. A. O. Essien as custodial of funds to pay them. Or that a window of opportunity to receive direct support was open for them to be independent and free from supervision, removing thereby any suspicion perhaps they might have harbored about not receiving adequately or correct amounts sent. This point, arguably, may have been a compelling reason that triggered them to disassociate themselves from C. A. O. Essien who shared their direct supporters contact information with hem.

The Diestelkamp, or anti-movement, group appeared appealing and an enticing avenue of providing direct support, without a middleman. The position eliminated any supervision, except directly to the supporting congregation, which was absent from the scene, and to the recipients in a country where scammers abound. The anti-movement group believed the Bible but rejected denominational churches and their doctrines. We have many points in common, but as the two protagonists, the prima donnas of the anti-movement, they felt more laws and rules were needed to keep the brethren in line. They forbade things God had not forbidden. They were usually regarded as factious; that is, they stirred up controversy and confusion among brethren, thereby becoming divisive. "If they could not prevail to have their own way, they would divide a congregation and lead away those who fell under their influence."[109]

These two individuals jumped ship, becoming the polarizing agents of the anti-movement.

I hope that liberals and conservatives desist from splitting hairs over teachings that have no direct bearing on human salvation. Rather than be engulfed in methodical issues that cause dissension, "All Christians need Luther's four gospel slogans (*sola gratia*—solely grace, *solar fide*—solely faith, *solo Christo*—solely Christ, *sola scriptura*—solely scripture), capped by Calvin's persistent admonition that all things result in the glory of God."[110]

Another group, "the Anabaptists, teach us the difference between being citizens of a worldly state and belonging to the kingdom of God, while reminding us that we must personally choose to follow Jesus as Lord and Master, and to include in church organization and worship only that which the Scripture permits and authorized."[111] When the stage for battle is drawn, the result is an orthodoxy that shrivels and embitters rather than fostering spiritual health or a sense of collective harmony.

Sunday Unogwu Onah

Brother Sunday Unogwu Onah participated in the World Bible School under the tutelage of Mrs. Goldie Smith of Upland Church of Christ in California. Through the overseas biblical instruction, he grasped relevant information about the church, its establishment, doctrine, and governance. Sunday Unogwu Onah learned to teach, preach, and organize churches, based on the theoretical concepts he learned. He said, "I became the preacher for the Makurdi, Benue State and during the next four years, I organized WBS seminars, and area follow-up teacher training. As part of this ministry, I traveled to seven other towns and villages in Benue preaching each Lord's Day."[112]

Brother Onah left Nigeria in 1997 to attend the Southern California School of Evangelism, and in his absence, Brother Isaiah Adikwu, his protégée from Otukpo, took care of the work at Makurdi. His curriculum vitae indicated his keen desire to return to "begin a comprehensive training of area workers to minister to nearly sixty congregations in Benue State. In correlation with WBS, I will be organizing lectureships, seminars, and workshops to focus on bringing students to conversion to Christ."[113] These were the factors that enhanced the growth of the church in Benue State.

Brother Onah was an ardent and devoted worker, whose life and his wife, Bassey, helped advance the numerical growth of churches in Benue State. His regular monthly reports to the leaders of Upland Church in California reflected statistical information on the enrollee converts of the WBS. For example, in 1998, the total number of congregations in Benue was fifty-eight, but it was reported: Since becoming a Christian and through the WBS, Brother Onah has converted 98 denominational leaders Between 1993 and 1997; enrolled 15,205 WBS students and of these, 9,075 completed the training. Through Brother Onah's efforts, along with several others who shared the teaching and preaching responsibilities with him, "some congregations were also planted in Kogi State (those areas that were parts of Benue State.) This was before the creation of Kogi State, and these were:

- "one congregation in Ankpa Local Government Area,
- three congregations in Olamaboro Local Government Area,
- one congregation in Dekina Local Government Area, and
- fifteen congregations planted by other ministers."[114]

As was evident in other communities of Nigeria, Brother Onah explained that the method of evangelization used was personal evangelism, which encouraged members to bring their neighbors. "The use of media advertisement, group meetings, open-air preaching, and indoor lectureships were established in different zones for Bible studies. Workshops, seminars, and youth forums were conducted solely aimed at evangelization, individual outreach programs,"[115] designed to strengthen preachers and the general membership in the Local Government Areas, were adopted as strategies for conversion and stabilization of churches.

Chukwu Okpep Uaori Ogwuru

Because of poor economic conditions, Ogwuru was not educated beyond sixth grade. Through self-determination, however, he taught himself to read beyond a high school level. Soon after his conversion in 1951 by Brother C. A. O. Essien, Brother Ogwuru enrolled in the three-month Bible training program at Ikot Usen and later was admitted to the Bible Training School, Ukpom Abak. Upon completing one year at Ukpom, Ogwuru transferred to the Onicha Ngwa Bible School, where he finally completed the two-year biblical studies.

Linguistically, he was naturally more conversant in his native tongue than the English language and was, therefore, in his element where Igbo was readily spoken. Upon graduating, he returned to Ogboteo Ozuitam in Isiala Ngwa, in Aba He was a parcel of energy, visiting villages and most sections of the Aba metropolis, teaching at street junctions, conducting open-air lectures, and publicizing the name of Christ and his church. Brother Ogwuru was an indefatigable minister, establishing churches in the Eyimba city of Aba, including surrounding towns.

When the financial support of local churches from America was threatened to be withdrawn, he taught his members and the churches not to be dependent on external support but to be self-sufficient by supporting their own preachers, as well as undertaking the support of an evangelistic campaign, a position that did not, at the time, quite resonate with many churches. He was a great warrior and leader for the Lord.

Owukiabo Elkanah Young

Brother Young, as he was dearly called, came at a time when the church needed men of meager fortune. Through his international marketing business, he invested in benevolence and the publishing of religious doctrine materials. He was bold and knowledgeable in the scriptures through self-study, and he wanted people to know the value of believing in God. He was an independent thinker, brave, charismatic, and always ready to challenge or discuss biblical topics that deviated from "thus said the Lord." He was a very warm-hearted, hospitable Christian who distributed a reasonable amount of his earnings to those in need.

Brother Young attended Northwestern University in Evanston, Illinois, where he earned his degree as a certified public accountant (CPA). In Nigeria, he met Brother Raphael Williams, now Edet Eduok. Through a series of biblical discussions, he compared what he heard from Eduok to other religious teachings, which were different and in opposition to what Eduok taught him. Without hesitation, he decided to give himself to Christ. This action made him a rebel, which meant going against the wishes of his parents. He immediately began to study the scriptures assiduously. Through his personal private studies, with help from Brother Eduok and other preachers in the area, he felt ready to launch into the field as a defender of the faith.

As an advocate of the New Testament church, he believed in the oneness of the church and the governance of local churches through eldership. He was a strong believer in Christian education. Brother Young became the chairman of the Board of Trustees, Nigeria, a corporation established only to meet the federal government policy; it had no power or control over other independent churches. With a wide range of interests, he published the books such as, "*What You Need to Know about Unity, Peace, Marriage, Reincarnation, Holy Spirit, Satan, and the Mystic World.*"[116]

Wendell Broom

In 1954, J. Harold and Howard Horton were responsible for Wendell Broom's considering serving as a missionary in Nigeria. He graduated from Abilene College (now University) with a bachelor's degree and later received an appointment to preach for the Tenth and Francis Church in Oklahoma City, Oklahoma, for ten years. Upon completing his full-time service as missionary to Nigeria, he combined advanced academic studies with missionary activities in a professorship position with Abilene University, a position that spanned a period of twelve years. While at Abilene as a professor, he visited Nigeria and other West African countries intermittently from 1974 to 1996.

When Wendell Broom arrived Nigeria in 1955, he lived at Ikot Usen, Ibiono, a community many thought was an unimproved section of the country, without electricity, public water, or a good road leading to the village. Being asked if he felt frightened to live in the area, he remarked, "People are frightened by what they do not understand, but [I am] loved and welcomed by Ikot Usen people [and] strongly befriended by house workers."[117] He said he established a wholesome relationship with preachers like Fearless Akpan, J. U. Akpan, G. M. Ntuk, and Essien Ekanem, all of whom made significant contributions to conversions, planting new churches, visiting, and encouraging weak churches. Though he lived at Ikot Usen, he visited villages and towns in the old Calabar province to nurture and train preachers, in addition to the concentrated teaching assignment at Ukpom Bible Training College.

He continued to plow and surge into unknown territories, teaching, lecturing, and debating unbelieving denominational preachers. Their influence and the truths propounded caused many to pay close attention to the unfamiliar teachings that challenged the consciences of diligent seekers. It was inevitable that many accepted Christ. When Broom was asked for the factors that contributed to and enhanced the growth of churches, he pointed to the following: "Very strong zeal by the Efik-Ibibio preachers, their eagerness and encouragement to plant churches, to care for the spiritual needs, and dependence on God."[118]

Conversely, he pointed to factors that helped retard church growth—shortage of preachers, lack of education, inadequate preparation, as well as the inability of local churches to actively generate good income to pay their preachers or to participate in evangelism, which was a personal concern. With regard to education, he wrote about some of the nationals who were actively involved in the administrative institutions—men like Solomon Aquaowo, who was the secretary to several of the missionaries; David Anako, a teacher and chaplain at the Ukpom Bible Training Institute, Ukpom; Chief Okon E. Mkpong of the Nigerian Christian Institute, Uyo; and Brother Agu of the Biblical Institute Jos, He also wrote about me, as I was the principal at the Nigerian Christian Secondary School, including the Christian Secondary Technical College, Oyubia Town, Oron.

Wendell Broom was visionary. In August 1977, he conceived the role Africa would play in God's plan to plant churches of born-again believers in all the world. Continuing in that vein, he wrote,

> "We have also heard that some of you [Africans] have made a covenant with some of us [Americans] to move towards each other in preaching, teaching, and planting churches with the goal and dream to meet in the Central African Republic by the help of God."[119]

This dream was a fait accompli when one of the African Jamboree assembled for a collaborative strategic venture for the spread of the gospel. When the Jamboree was launched, Wendel Broom distinguished himself in his devotion to the cause by frequently returning to the field to see how the brethren were doing. In his secular letter to Nigerian ex-workers in 1997, sent to rally the support of the brethren, he said that he wanted them to consider the need to develop a chronological historical record of events among the churches. He wrote,

> "In my visit to Ukpom in August this year [1997], I was delighted to see the promising young leaders of the churches there, by conservative estimate, there were probably 2,200 churches of Christ in Nigeria. There are medical doctors, nurses, businessmen, political leaders, elders, deacons, preachers, people with college level education (with a surprising

number of master's and doctoral degrees).
Our days of the "bush boys" are gone.
Ukpom is now offering the first three
years of the BA degree and beginning of
a master's degree. And incidentally, some
of the sons of men you taught are now
struggling to find the $500 it takes for a
year of graduate study at the Universities
of Calabar, Uyo, Port Harcourt and many
others. What a great future lies before
God's people. our sons and daughters in
the faith!"[120]

The church grew rapidly, with numerous baptisms,
through the efforts of the Nigerian preachers and
American missionaries between 1948 and 1951, prior to
the arrival of the first two missionaries. Wendell Broom
indicated that Brother C. A.O. Essien baptized 1,642
during the five months from August to December. In
May, 340 more were baptized. In the first six weeks of
Howard Horton's residency, there were a total of 1,500
to 2,000, more converts than we ever had experienced.

Willie Cato

The story on the history of the Church of Christ in
Nigeria would be incomplete without the selfless sacrifices

that Willie Cato made on numerous occasions for the sole purpose of training workers. Early in 1955, Willie Cato came to a realization, along with the members of the Board of Trustees of the Nigerian Christian Schools (later renamed African Christian Schools): the only way Christians could intelligently combat negative name-calling and religious slander was through education.

To break through the pseudo-impenetrable wall of religiosity and snobbishness, Christians deserved a sound educational environment, based on Christian principles. Cato's experience at the Nashville Christian Institute more than prepared him for the task, and, like Moses, he had seen poverty at its best. Students were denied admission into existing Christian institutions based purely on racial discrimination—skin pigmentation. Willie Cato served as the president of African Christian Schools (1967–1972) and was the director of Happy Hills Boys' Ranch (Home). Among the multitude of tasks that Brother Cato shouldered was the responsibility for fund-raising, visiting churches, and soliciting individual members for funds to aid the mission effort of African Christian Schools. He was exemplary in his genuine concern as he traveled long distances, visited schools to recruit Christian missionaries, and talked to many who might contribute to the cause.

A regular-contributing elderly sister, who was bedridden, asked Brother Cato to visit with her. We drove more than a hundred miles to visit the sister. After exchanging greetings and reminiscences, Cato asked her how she was feeling. She expressed concern for the work and, in her feeble, weak voice, asked Cato how the work was progressing. Cato informed her that there was great progress and that several missionaries had visited Nigeria. We knew she was tired and perhaps could not entertain conversation. Before we said prayer to God to sustain her and said goodbye, she reached under her pillow, with her eyes closed, pulled out an envelope that contained her welfare check, and gave it to Willie Cato, saying, "This is the last check I shall collect. Use it for the work."

Both Willie Cato and I stood shocked, gazing at the frail body of a valiant disciple. We looked at each other, pondering the significance of the check from a sister who was, perhaps, dying. This was on a Saturday; on Monday, Brother Cato received a telephone call that informed him that the sister had died. God still works in mysterious ways, performing his wonders, where we neither know nor have control over our destinies. What was apparent was that Christians like her, in many congregations across the United States or in the world, who cannot physically go to mission fields, have dedicated themselves to indirect teaching and preaching, even, for some, in their bedridden conditions. That was also Sister Poston, who was blind, at Avalon Church of Christ in Los Angeles, who gave bountifully to the Nigerian work. What an enduring, powerful message. What a faith in God.

Rees and Patti Bryant

Figure 19

Missionaries at Onicha Ngwa Bible College

Rees and Patti Bryant spent more than five years at the Onicha Ngwa Bible Training School, teaching, preaching, and leading as many as possible to Christ, in many cities and towns of Abia State, Owerri, Enugu, and other sanctuaries of Igboland. Rees actively participated in the establishment of the Nigerian Christian Hospital from 1982 to 1984 and worked in Plateau State under adverse conditions.

In January 1982, the Bryants were packed and ready to return to Nigeria, this time leaving their children behind in the United States. Rees explained,

> "As often happens when leaving loved
> ones behind, I took each child off a little

distance and gave him/her a final word
of blessings. I can't remember what I said
to each of them, but I remember what I
said to our oldest, who had several serious
relationships and a broken engagement by
then: "Sara Jo, you have proved that you
can be cautious; now you need to prove
that you can be decisive." Five years later,
she did so by marrying Bruce Martin
Disterhoft."[121]

All of this was in anticipation of the loneliness that
missionaries and loved ones in distant countries, away
from home, encounter. This time, upon returning to
Nigeria, the Bryants traveled with a group of young
American missionaries, Mary and Kim Luallen, Tim
and Belinda Curtis, and three bachelors: David Little,
Craig Trudgen, and Clarence Wilson. These were
joined later by Kenneth and Deborah Klein, Wallace
and Tammy Sutter, and Irving and Ronda Everson, who
were housed temporarily in different homes of members
of the church.

On Saturday, January 9, 1982, they boarded a DC-
10 airplane that had to be de-iced. Bryant related the
frightening experience that most who fly, encounter:

After we were seated comfortably, and the
stewards had served our drinks, we settled

in for a direct flight to Lagos. An hour out over the ocean, it happened! Our airplane went into a most sudden drop. The drinks flew up to the ceiling, passengers started screaming. We thought we were going to die, I put my head down and prayed, "Lord, save our souls. Take care of our children. After the plane had dropped about 250 feet, it hit the bottom of the air pocket very abruptly, almost like we had hit a runway."[122]

With the buffeting and shaking of the plane like a leaf in a storm, Rees felt that the pilot had lost control. Soon, however, the turbulence subsided, and as he checked on the other missionaries, a European lady, who had overheard his prayer, said, "I was not."

Rees responded, "Lady, do you remember what happened to the Christians in Rome during the persecution, when they (Christians) were fed to the lions and burned at the stake?"[123]

Unless one flies often, Bryant's experience might be hard to imagine, especially when one is thousands of miles from home. How to deal with frightful experiences like this are not taught in seminaries, but one must be prepared, mentally and emotionally, to expect the unexpected and to adjust and trust in God.

While waiting to fly from Lagos airport to Kano, Rees remarked, "An official-looking man boarded [the] plane and announced that there was no room for all the luggage on the plane." Having been in Nigeria for years, Rees knew this was a ploy. "Since I knew he was simply trying to get us to pay him a bribe, I said, 'We will just go to Kano on this plane and wait for our things to catch up with us.' After several attempts, the officer gave up, and we left."[124]

At Jos, the internship missionaries were posted to schools in different directions. They were employed by the Plateau State Government to teach Christian religious knowledge and other subjects in the public schools. From their station, Tim and Belinda Curtis were back to complain about the overwhelming and unaccustomed dirt, grime, smells, noise, and terrible poverty they saw everywhere. "They were posted to a third-floor apartment that was filthy, and it had a two-burner kerosene stove."[125]

The next day, both Tim and Belinda, who were young and inexperienced with people in poor and disadvantaged African society and without the conveniences of the Western world, were at Rees's door, having spent the night in tears. They told Rees they had no idea that things would be as they were. Of course, they had seen pictures of the deplorable living conditions, but it was hard to describe.

One must have the heart of a lion to be a missionary in Nigeria, particularly in the villages but even in the so-called townships, where conditions are one level higher but still without amenities. Prior to his return, Rees said that Tim had made a derogatory comment about one of the nicer parts of Jos.

"What did you expect?" Rees had asked him.

"I thought it would be like Ireland," Tim said.

Many who impulsively jump on the bandwagon for a missionary adventure do more damage to the course when they develop selective-hearing syndrome. Rees was patient and kind, a friend of many, exhibiting, on every occasion, the true spirit of a Christian.

Bill and Gerry Nicks

Figure 20
Missionaries at Onicha Ngwa Bible College

The news concerning the Nigerian evangelistic work from 1959 to 1962 gained prominence among the brotherhood. Colleges and churches reporting frequently about the receptivity and the progress of the work. Bill Nicks felt ready to do his part. He had varied experiences, both academic and religious, and had earned an associate degree from Freed Hardeman College (now University), a bachelor's degree from Memphis State University, and a master's degree from Abilene Christian University. Bill said, "After I had been preaching in the US for twelve years and helping establish new congregations in my local work, I visited Howard Horton in Nashville after his return from Nigeria, where he showed us pictures of Nigeria and encouraged us to go and help because he was not returning to Nigeria. He urged me to consider beginning a training program among the Igbos since some students [from that area] were at Ukpom, and they had no missionary working in the Igbo communities."[126]

Bill and his family arrived in Nigeria in October 1955, taking residence temporarily at Ukpom, while preparing to embark upon the new phase of work in Igbo. From Ukpom, they took Brother Stephen Okoronkwo, a multilingual national, and Anike, both students at Ukpom Bible College. Stephen's transforming demeanor, versatility, and fluency in the languages made him an excellent translator and guide.

There was no housing in the area, but through God's providence, the district officer (DO), whom they had found at Aba, was congenial and friendly. Bill said, "The divisional officer allowed us to have the former rest house, a housing unit normally used by government officers during court sessions. They were no longer using it, so we "inherited" it. We lived in it until we could build our own house on the land at Ntigha Onicha Ngwa, where we rented fifteen acres of land."[127]

In fulfillment of their desire to stabilize the work in Igbo area, the training of preachers was paramount. In addition to Stephen and Anike, Josiah Akandu and Ndukwe and Reginald Okoreke became the first second-year students, the freshmen students were selected from prospects who came in great numbers. We selected forty candidates, some of whom became great preachers among the Igbo men, such as Jacob Achinefo, Daniel Ogbonna, and Reuben Iheanacho. Chuku Ogwuru began preaching nearby and was a great help [and a dependable and loyal Christian].

Their ministry effort was not localized; villages like Onicha Ngwa, Nlagu, and the churches nearby—Itungwa, Umohia, and Aba, were included in their evangelistic endeavors.

Before they arrived in the area, Bill said that missionaries like Howard Horton, Elvis Huffard, and

Burney Bawcom had done a little work among the Igbos. He enumerated some of the churches in the different local government areas and villages—for example, there was a church in Onicha Ngwa, Itu Ngwa, Akoli Aba, Ohanze Aba, Umuodosi, and four churches in the Uzuakoli area and four in Umohia. There were about ten churches in the Aba area. Owerri, had several churches in Mbaise, one of which was in Ife Nowutu. The presence of devoted and committed missionary ministers, who were scripturally versed and knew the social and religious underpinnings of the communities, helped in the rapid conversions of many. Nothing could stop them. They now ventured into Enugu, the Coal City and the capital of the then-Eastern Region, where they established two churches and another one at Nsukka. Taking temporary residence at Ukpom, Bill said that the first churches established in Igbo area were started by Howard Horton, et al.

Chuku Ogwuru, David Ibekwe, Josiah Akandu, Josiah Nwadioha, and A. K. Owusoro were preachers from the Uzuakoli area. Akandu later took a teaching appointment at the School of Preaching at Onicha Ngwa, as did D. D. Isonguyo. The Onicha Ngwa Bible Training School was started in 1957, a school Bill pioneered, while they lived in the courthouse until they had their own building.

The school was near a stream of water for the students to use; it was also near Aba, a commercial center, where the students could do their shopping, with an easy transportation connection. The first teachers at the school were James Finney, D. D. Isonguyo, Josiah Akandu, Bill Nicks, and, later, Stephen Okoronkwo, with a total of forty-three students. From the community, Ntigha Onicha Ngwa, the school leased fifteen acres from Chief Thomas Ebere for approximately thirty dollars per year, plus gifts of cloth, yams, pineapples, etc., as payment for the ninety-nine-year lease. Nicks, with his youthful zeal, was the brains behind the establishment of Onicha Ngwa Bible School.

Henry Farrar, MD

Figure 21

Henry Farrar, MD, an angel in human clothing

Dr. Henry Farrar was an unusual person who saw caring for suffering humanity and the sick as a practical demonstration of Christ's love. For him, healing the sick was not simply a reaction to the Hippocratic Oath but an important feature of Christ's mission, which deserved obedience with practical application. Christ attended to and healed diverse diseases. The apostles were empowered to heal the sick as a means of authenticating God's presence in their ministry. Henry Farrar, by emulating Christ, made an enormous difference in the lives of the people he met, taught, and medically treated. He had a great capacity to relieve the sick, both physically and spiritually, in their brokenness.

Figure 22   **Figure 23**

As a student at Harding College (now University), he intended to enter China as a medical missionary, but friends persuaded him to consider Nigeria, where he could be effective, with endless possibilities.

Ukpom Bible Training College started in 1954 as a prelude to entering Nigeria, when Bill Nicks reported the existence of forty-five Igbo and three hundred Efik-Ibibio churches. In 1957, Onicha Ngwa Bible Training College began, and its beginning bore the need for Brother Farrar to consider a vibrant mission trip to Nigeria.

In 1963, Brother Farrar and Jack Sinclair, from West End Church in Nashville, visited Nigeria to select a location for launching the medical dream for which he had prayed and yearned for many years. In 1964, Henry and his wife, Grace, as well as Iris Hays (Savio) and Nancy Petty Kraus, began their medical mission at Onicha Ngwa, which culminated in January 1965 with the first outpatient clinic. The progress and future of the clinic, which would soon become a hospital, was bright. The confidence of the chiefs and people of the community made the process for acquiring the 119 acres of land on a ninety-nine–year lease between the village of Ntigha Onicha Ngwa, Nlagu, Uwuwaoma, and the Church of Christ an epoch-making event. John Beckloff, Rees Bryant, J. O. Akandu, Chukwu Oguru, John Ebere, Benjamin Ikanne, Henry Farrar, and I were signatories, representing the Church of Christ.

From 1965 to '67, Farrar wrote of the amazing blessing in the construction of five buildings, like five floors of an American hospital, and a thirty-foot water tower were completed under the supervision of Anthony Agali. With numerous intervening events, the major one, being the civil war conflict between Nigeria and Biafra, all resident medical personnel evacuated the country for safety reasons. "When the missionary workers departed the country, the hospital was supervised and operated by Nigerians, like Moses Okpara and Dr. Edward Akpabio of Ukana, Ikot Ekpene."[128]

Soon after the cessation of conflict, the Red Cross used the Nigerian Christian Hospital (NCH) as a clinic and feeding station. Dr. Farrar narrated succinctly many of the events after the return of missionaries to rehabilitate the hospital. In 1970, Dr. Farrar, Dr. Derek Belgrave, and Moses Oparah, who received the support of West End Church of Christ in Nashville, Tennessee, and the Christian Council of Nigeria, teamed to rehabilitate the hospital.

Dr. Farrar said, "In 1971, Dr Maurice and Johnnie Hood arrived to lend hands. Dr. Hood was a resident surgeon from the University of New York, New York Dr. Bob Whittaker, nurse Nancy Petty Kraus, and many others worked long hours at the Nigerian Christian Hospital."[129]

In 1972, the African Christian Hospital Foundation was established at Lubbock, Texas, (with Rees Bryant as president), principally to solicit funds and recruit prospective medical personnel. To broaden the scope of medical services at the hospital, the following accounts were provided by Dr. Henry Farrar. In 1972–1980, Dr. and Mrs. Hood, Dr. Jesse Paul, Dr. Ann Weaver, Dr. and Mrs. Charles Graham, and Dr. Jeff Jones of Texas; Dr. Phil Bryan of Oklahoma; Dr. Howard Ausherman of Florida; Dr. Marvin Fowler of Missouri; Dr. Frank Black of Indiana; Dr. and Mrs. Chas Hawes of Ohio; and nurses Patty Woods (Wilson) of Arkansas and Lola Bowen of Georgia volunteered to work part-time at the hospital. This was a great time for the hospital.

> Interested church elders, leaders, preachers, and friends flocked to Nigeria to witness, to encourage, and to teach in as many churches as they had the opportunity. We saw in action the words of Victor Hugo, who said in *Les Misérables*, 'Man lives more by affirmation than by bread.' Those who came had no bread (riches) but gave of themselves, bringing sunshine that helped invigorate and brighten the emotion and spirit of the servants, both American missionaries, and the Nigerian churches. There were many of these, but we can only mention these few.

Dr. Farrar, who was already a resident doctor at the hospital, along with other missionaries, invited people to visit Nigeria regularly. Sister Patti Mattox Bryant, who also attended one of these lectures, observed her father, Dr. F. W. Mattox, the president of Lubbock Christian University, in the one-day lectureship at Ukpom Bible School. The lectureship included Henry Farrar, the leader of the team; Douglas Lawyer; Joe Cross; and Rees Bryant, as members of the American visiting team.

In her book, *Divine Choreography*, Patti wrote, Daddy was given the topic "The Place of Education in a Free Nation, with enough latitude that he could say anything he wanted. The men who reserved the Town Hall in Aba and distributed 1,250 printed invitations, targeted the educated Nigerians in Aba" Prominent Nigerians like the division officer Mr. F. T. Ella, and Ekukinam A. Bassey, the former commissioner in the foreign office, supervised seventeen thousand Nigerians in European universities. "The missionaries and the Nigerian evangelists collaboratively sought every avenue to advertise and to expose the church to the public."[130]

Sister Bryant reported a situation of dialectic value, perhaps more so to the Nigerians than the Americans, and she subtitled her thoughts, "The Best Sermon My Father Ever Made."[131]

> "As great as all Daddy's sermons and lectures were that week, there was one "sermon" that probably made the

greatest impression of all. It happened one morning when our septic tank began to back up into the bathtub and toilet. Horror of horror! What a time for this to happen! I was at a loss, but Daddy knew just what to do. He rolled up his sleeves, found a shovel, and began to dig. As he shoveled out the disgusting contents, a small, astonished group of Nigerians gathered in amazement. "No, sir! No! You must not do this!" They felt ashamed that a visitor of Brother Mattox's stature would so humble himself to do such a task. [These were men with a false sense of importance—egomaniacs—and such people in Nigerian society do not generally perform what they regard as menial labor.] "As they protested, Daddy just kept working until the job was finished. That was my daddy. He was just as comfortable with a shovel as he was behind a lectern in the Town Hall. The missionaries had presented Daddy as someone of great importance, but in that one act, Daddy showed them, and all of us, what true greatness is."[132]

Not only greatness, but humility—a lesson Nigerians must learn, as Christ taught us to humble ourselves in the sight of God and man.

In 1963, an incident of similar nature occurred when my wife, Sister LaVera E. Otoyo, was the principal of Independence High School, Ukana, Ikot Ekpene. She enjoyed and had a love for farming as she realized the need to grow food. One day, while working in the farm after school, the final-year students in the nearby dormitory saw her digging in the soil. They were surprised to see someone in such a "high" position as the principal of a school working on the farm, a task usually reserved for servants. Many of the girls rushed over and took the spade from her, saying, "Madam, big people don't work in farms." Mrs. Otoyo, at about eight months pregnant, was indeed big. She replied, "I am big all right," but she could not tell whether they meant physically or in academic and positional status. Most Nigerians, once they acquire a modicum of education, feel exempted from manual labor. The students, nevertheless, admonished her that educated college graduates in Nigeria and someone in her position as an administrator of a high school should not farm. With her own characteristic humor, she chided, "That's why all of you are hungry all the time—because you refuse to work."[133]

This was an honest and direct chastisement that I felt the students needed to hear. For many years, friends of the Nigerian mission evangelistic work continued swooping (they came in great numbers), descending like kits to the prey into the country. Many apprentice students from colleges and universities came, but it wasn't as spectators in a basketball or soccer game, watching and enjoying themselves, nor as tourists, whose main objective is to be entertained and for which the thrill and excitement of the occasion is central. The missionary apprentices came with a purpose to serve and to share their lives with the dejected—those without Christ, helpless without hope. Some came to provide medical assistance, others to preach or teach, and others still as catalysts, helping the missionaries as they worked among the churches.

This was a great time of awakening regarding medical attention for the people, who came in great numbers. Some who were in need of treatment slept in the corridors and on floors of the hospital, and some hadn't eaten for an entire day. Dr. Farrar observed, "Each patient will have one to four or five family members with him [or her, so] these family members are on the verandas outside the ward, and the children sleep under the patient's bed."[134] They did not mind the inclement, hot, humid tropical weather. News of the quality of service, the compassionate dispensing of medical care, and the manner exhibited by the hospital personnel continued to spread into many villages. The sick, with varied illnesses, arrived, many without money to pay for their treatment. The hospital became a beacon of hope for the poor and helpless.

With the growing need at the hospital and the demands on it, Dr. Farrar and a few others at Christian Hospital devoted themselves to recruiting. Dr. Farrar wrote that between 1980 and 1982,

> "Dr. Robert and Debbie Mahaffey and their four children begin work at the Nigerian Christian Hospital (NCH.) Nurse Janice Bingham does outstanding work and is designing the new pediatric ward, to be named for Emmett and Nell Bryant. Dr. Geo and Linda Robertson of Tennessee and Dr. David Staggs of Arkansas, with Nigerian doctors like Dr. Azikiwe Ikeorha, kept the hospital operating, despite tribal warfare and armed robbers nearby, escalating inflation, and political unrest.[135]

Another event of importance was the appointment of Brother Glenn Boyd as the president of the African Christian Hospital Foundation (ACHF), a move that reflected a broad-based perspective of the ACHF, not as a parochial Nigerian-based operation but inclusive of other African countries. As professional workers arrived, the medical care expanded. Nancy Clark led twenty-one nurses from Harding University. Sonny Parkhill was engaged in the construction and supervision of buildings. He also taught the Bible. Dr. Terry and Linda Olivet of Birmingham, Alabama, and Dr. Glenn Browning of Missouri served in the surgery at NCH. Others who came to give encouragement to the medical needs of the hospital were Drs. Richard Burt of Dallas, Texas, and Jim Bratton of Oklahoma, who began the first dental clinic at the hospital. Dr. Brian and Susan Camazine served in surgery for the first of their three visits. Brian developed cerebral malaria and was treated successfully with quinine. Dr Farrar wrote that Bob and Michele Bentley of Texas and Brent and Kay Magner served in the administration with other recruits, like Lori Sutherland and Linda Ferguson of Texas, Gem Spence of California, and Becky Smith, who served as nurses. They exhibited their love in obedience to the gospel message, coupled with their compassion to alleviate the suffering of many.

Articulating his dreams, as well as the motivation that prompted him as a naturally gifted teacher and ardent believer in Christ, Farrar wrote, since Jesus' followers are sent as the Father sent Him, Matt. 4:23 applies to us: "Jesus went throughout Galilee, teaching in their synagogues, preaching the good news of the kingdom, and healing every disease and sickness among the people. True, He had miraculous knowledge, we must strive to follow Him in preaching. Since the lack of miraculous power does not stop us from imitating Jesus' preaching, in the same way lack of miracle power does not excuse us from the necessity of healing. We cannot duplicate his preaching or his healing, but we must come as close to these things as we can as we walk in His footsteps.[136]

Marshall Keeble (The Revered Veteran Soldier of the Cross)

Marshall Keeble was the indomitable, highly renowned, and respected African American minister, whose legacy transcended racial cleavages. He opened the road, bridging the gap that divided whites and blacks within the church. He was not a politician to champion the cause of equality; having lived under segregated conditions himself, he bore the pain, the humiliation, and the demoralizing pangs of racial injustice. Keeble was born in Murfreesboro, Tennessee, in 1878 and started preaching in 1897, with the encouragement of his father in-law, S. D. W. Womack.

Brother J. E. Choate, the author of *Roll Jordan Roll*, wrote that Keeble converted more people than any preacher, black or white, of the Church of Christ. He never attended college, and in several cities and towns where he preached, Keeble quipped that he never went to college "to get his brain expanded." The contradiction in this wisecrack and his establishment of the Nashville

(Preachers) Training Institute cannot be misunderstood as a negation of education. Choate then added, "No one could come close to his ability in presenting the gospel as he did." What was unique about Keeble was that people flocked in large numbers to hear him wherever he was, in any town, "not because he was a Negro, but because they wanted to hear what he had to say."[137]

He had an uncommon way of making his illustrations through anecdotes and parables, mixed with homespun humor that was easily understandable and appealing. He was one of the pillars of the restoration movement, along with pioneers like Alexander Campbell, Barton W. Stone, Tolbert Fanning, Samuel Robert Cassius, and David Lipscomb. Most of his evangelistic preaching was financed by white brethren, particularly A. M. Burton. Though he never attended college to have his "brain expanded," a phenomenon caused by the existing ignominious racial discrimination, he felt that for young Afro-Americans to be successful in the ministry, they needed a better education.

He pioneered the establishment of the Nashville Christian Institute in 1940 as a night school and, later, in 1942, as a school for young African American Christians. This was a school for young adults who were denied admission to any of the existing Christian institutions of higher learning. Willie Cato succeeded Marshall Keeble as the president of the Nashville Christian Institute, and they worked closely as a team for eight years, until the school closed.

Reflecting on the cordial relationship that existed between them, Keeble wrote, "I will always be glad that it was my privilege to recommend him [Willie Cato] to urge him to become President."[138] Reacting to the mutually beneficial relationship between Keeble and Cato, Choate wrote, "No other white person has worked as long in a daily personal contact with Marshall Keeble as Willie Cato." As a mark of endearment, Willie Cato called Marshall Keeble "Pap," which was out of genuine love and respect. To reciprocate, Keeble called Cato "son."[139]

In 1962, a few individuals, who felt Keeble could be of influence and inspiration to Churches of Christ around the world, recommended he visit Nigeria. Lucien Palmer, who wanted Keeble to travel, discussed plans for the trip with Brother Burton, who was vehemently opposed to Keeble's undertaking such a trip because of Keeble's advanced age, coupled with the rigors of traveling. Keeble and Burton were great friends, but "A. M. Burton was dead set against Keeble going and felt he should not go. [He] told Keeble, 'they will kill you; you are worth too much to the church to be running around all over the world taking all kinds of chances.'"[140]

Keeble said his old friend Burton had tears in his eyes. Realizing in the back of his mind that Keeble could not be dissuaded, he "reached in the back pocket for a thousand dollars to give on the trip." After touring other parts of the world, Brothers Keeble and Lucien Palmer finally reached Ukpom, Abak, Akwa Ibom State, Nigeria, where the first Bible school was established. From Ukpom, they visited the Asutan Ekpe Church of Christ for a welcome reception, given in Keeble's honor.

Keeble preached daily, exhorting, encouraging, and inspiring the members at Ikot Usen, where the church was first started in Nigeria by Brother C. A. O. Essien; fifty-five souls were converted. He spoke in marketplaces and by the riverside to teachers and students at the Bible schools. Considering his age, he was relentless and untiring, making known God's power and blessings during the period Brothers Palmer and Houston Ezell were with him. He observed the elaborate "fine" schools and hospitals of the Catholic Church and other religious establishments. Keeble perceptibly observed, "I tell you, fellows—that's what is wrong with the Church of Christ. These churches get here fifty years ahead of us, get these children and train them, and line up the people and indoctrinate them. Then we send two missionaries over here and try to head them off."[141]

Keeble was an encourager in every way. He was at home with himself and with the people who loved and respected him as a father. At his farewell party, which was attended by local government dignitaries, he was bestowed the highest honorary title of a chief, with all the rights and privileges fit for a king, and a walking cane, symbolizing his authority as a king. Yet he was no king and had no kingdom, except that he was the servant of the Most high God.

J. P. Sanders ("Into the Heart of Africa")

J. P. Sanders was a unique visitor in many ways. His rise from humble beginnings in Fort Worth, Texas, in 1906, to becoming a preacher at the Hillsboro Church of Christ in Nashville and later at the Canoga Valley Church in California was inspiring. He taught at David Lipscomb University (then College) and later at Pepperdine University, when Dr. Norvel Young was the president of Pepperdine University, with Sanders as one of the professors; both coauthored the publication, *The 20th Century Christian.*

Brother J. P. Sanders's narrative on his experiences in Nigeria in February 1965 was insightful. He reflected on the activities he felt made the Nigerian mission efforts successful. He made relational observations about Port Harcourt, the world's third-largest delta, exceeded only by the Nile and the Ganges Rivers. Brother Phillip Dunn, then the principal of the Bible College at Ukpom, met Sanders at the airport and then drove 102 miles on the rugged bush road to Ukpom. He described the tropical surroundings of the Bible College as clean, calm, and neat. He then described the three Nigerian teachers and American missionaries' residential quarters as "comfortable and well arranged."[142] There was a diesel power system that provided electrical current for about five hours each evening. "The refrigerators are operated by kerosene, and the cooking stoves are supplied with bottled butane gas." Health precautions were necessary for survival in a country that was infested with water-borne diseases. Without hygienic care for cooking and drinking water, one would suffer the consequences of an infectious disease that ultimately would inhibit missionary activity.

Sanders observed that the work of these "Christian people involves teaching, preaching, and serving in different ways" and often traveling within a radius of thirty to fifty miles. He noticed that the wives of the missionaries also taught classes to women and children in many villages and provided first-aid attention to those with boils, ulcers, dysentery, and cough, which were common ailments. "The missionaries serve around the clock and are likely to be called at any hour of the day or night to render assistance to someone in need."[143]

When Sanders visited the large open markets, he was impressed with the arrangement of the booths, most of which were covered with palm-leaf roofs, where seemingly hundreds of merchants show their wares of every kind and description. Haggling over the price as part of the well-established and expected method of buying impressed him. On Sunday, he went with Brother Phillip Dunn, along with a Nigerian interpreter, and he addressed a native audience with approximately two hundred in attendance. Directly in front of me was a great crowd of children dressed in (birth birthday suits.) "Above the age of ten, they dress, with few exceptions, as modestly as people do in America. Behind these children stood mothers with babies on their hips or slung on their backs, as well as fathers and grandparents. They listened intently, and at the conclusion of the service, there were ten who wanted to be baptized."[144]

This type of reaction typified the desire of many who wanted to accept the unadulterated gospel. Pivotal to the work was the alliance with the government for the church to recruit and provide Bible teachers for government schools. Sanders could see the opportunity for the church to teach the Bible and of providing Bible teachers so that the children in these schools would have a lesson in the Bible, which the government syllabus described as "moral instruction," each day.

Brother John Beckloff, who was the manager of the schools at the time, must have provided Sanders with the statistics of "twenty-five hundred students in the schools under his supervision. Brother Beckloff was also granted the privilege of providing Bible teachers in about forty-five other government schools, where seven thousand children received daily Bible instruction. Here, then, lay the great opportunity for the onslaught, a *coup de main* on the forces of spiritual darkness. Sanders, perceiving the opportunities for the church, added, there is hardly any way to estimate the value of this training to the country of Nigeria, to the development of Christian life in these students, and for the work of the Church."[145] People not only were captivated by his presence but took every opportunity to draw as much as they could from his pantheon of theological scholarship and wealth of experience. Sanders was sought after; he wrote of going "to preach in an evening service out in the bush that had been arranged by Brother Phillip Dunn. There was quite a large crowd assembled under a large palm roof. After the service, several people came to request that I visit. These requests come so frequently that it is impossible for the missionaries to go to all of the places to which they are asked."[146]

Though Brother J. P. Sanders did not go to Enugu, Brothers Keesee and Curry, with their families, came from Enugu to visit with him at Onicha Ngwa. The work these brethren began in that area resulted in the establishment of congregations, and over two hundred people were converted. One of the last to be baptized was Brother R. A. Item, a professor of zoology at the University of Nigeria, Nsukka.

Dayton Keesee

The arrival of Dayton Keesee, his wife, Ruth, and their children in March 19, 1964, increased the number of American missionaries in Nigeria. Dayton had come to know and identify with the Nigerian mission work through Douglas Lawyer, Jim Massey, and William (Bill) Curry. At Abilene Christian College, he contemplated entering a mission field upon earning a bachelor's degree, but he waited until he earned his master's degree at Butler University in Indianapolis.

As a leader of a mission group in 1950, at Abilene, Keesee felt that the influences in several lectures that were related to missions, mission reports, and especially his instructor, Dr. Homer Hailey, not only broadened his perspective on missions but prepared him for the reality of an arduous mission trip to Nigeria in 1964 (where he stayed until 1967). Upon arrival in Nigeria, he lived in Brother Rees Bryant's house at Onicha Ngwa, while Bryant was on leave in America. He met Brother Rufus Akitobi, who often interpreted for him. Keesee, along with Brothers Akitobi and Bill Curry, labored closely to open a new work in Enugu. Stephen Okoronkwo, Jacob Achinefu, Timothy Akpakpan, and Sunday Ekanem, men of incredibly high Christian values and well disciplined, contributed to the enhancement of the kingdom of God in Enugu.

In his reflections on teaching and preaching around Enugu for more than twenty-four months, Keesee said he helped to start forty congregations and helped "these babies in Christ with their problems and in their spiritual growth." Keesee felt that the common thread that constantly faced the church, particularly preachers, was carnality.[147] The interest in material matters that overrode spiritual concerns, coupled with government instability and their inability to help alleviate the citizens' internal political struggles and the gnawing self-interest among politicians indirectly affected the church.

Keesee, who arrived before the civil war, observed that interest in moral and spiritual matters prevailed. Some of the US-imported schisms and divisiveness, at one point, affected a sense of spiritual collectivism, thereby splintering the church into two groups—the liberals and the conservatives. The acquisition of wealth loomed large in the minds and motives of greedy preachers and members. Keesee felt that "wisdom from God on how to help may have been a great remedy."[148]

His view on the establishment of secular and religious institutions was, "If done to meet the spiritual and physical needs, God's wisdom is to be sought first, as recorded by Matthew, 'But seek yea first the kingdom of God and His righteousness, and all these things will be added unto you.'"[149] While teaching audiences, he observed that the "people were to seek New Testament principles and precepts." As he and others contemplated expanding to other states, like Benin (now Delta State), the brethren with a noncooperative, conservative, anti-group "did not want us to come into their territory, and rather than deal with that, our families moved to Enugu."[150]

Keesee dealt with the issues that affected the missionaries who were leaving the country. The political agitation in the East reached a crescendo on May 30, 1966, when the East seceded from the federal government of Nigeria to form what was known as Biafra.

On a trip from Lago to my village, when I heard the announcement on Radio Nigeria that war had been declared between Nigeria and Biafra, the federal government immediately imposed a formerly threatening economic blockade on Biafra. The blockade affected the East with no shipping or mail communication services. Keesee and others lived in the capital city of the Biafran government, a possible combat zone. Their lives would be threatened, should war erupt while they lived there. Keesee, however, did not feel threatened; if the situation became precarious, they would move to safe towns or cities. Unfortunately, this was not to be.

Keesee said later that their 'our primary reason for leaving was the economic blockade that now exists in Biafra. It is not possible to draw American funds into Biafra. What Nigerian money we had on hand was all we had to use. This would have soon tied our hands for effective work in Enugu Bible College, the radio work, and even in travel to work among the congregations.'

On June 4, 1967, they were told to evacuate their children and wives from Enugu, and they complied. "We had already discussed and prayed about the possibility of our being separated from each other."[151] Keesee and the McCluggages proceeded to Port Harcourt, although Ralph McCluggage still hoped to pursue the evangelistic work that already had gained momentum in the area. A few days later, as they stopped at Aba to see Gid Walters, two events happened: (1) the Walters had received word from the "contact man from the US Consulate, advising them to leave the next day; they were no longer evacuating just wives and children [but] urging all to leave. (2) They then wondered if the US government officials giving this information might know something that we didn't."[152]

On their way to Enugu, they had an accident with a truck, and their car was totaled. Consequently, they did not have adequate funds, the only money they had was in their pockets; the small amount they had in the car was stolen leaving them penniless. With such ill luck, their hands were tied unable to determine what action to make; they were forced to fast forward their decision much faster than they contemplated.

The US consulate's advice contributed to their decision to leave the country, as did missionaries at Ikot Usen, Ukpom-Abak, and Enugu, totaling twenty-four workers. The sudden evacuation of the missionaries dampened the spirits of indigenous evangelists, resulting

Eno O. Otoyo, Ed.D

in a temporary setback of the thrust of evangelistic work. After the missionaries left Nigeria, the unsavory report from America was that the Nigerian work was "dead." Churches and members would not hold on to the pledge to be faithful and unmovable amid adversity and external threats by the devil; it was therefore assumed that the evangelists were not mature or strong enough.

In other words, the church would not function without the presence of the Americans. It could be said that with the destructiveness and deaths by the thousands, families were severed. Consequently, the church could no longer survive because the American missionaries left Nigeria. This thought struck the Nigerian ministers and members like a lightning bolt. Numerous staunch, devoted Christians felt disappointed, dismayed, or betrayed over such a devastating opinion of the Nigerians and the work. For many years, the American missionaries were in the bushes, in market squares, and in trenches everywhere with Nigerians, under sun or rain. While proclaiming the reformative message, never did they suggest they were working for America. It was the banner of the gospel through Christ that they hoisted, not America, but the highest gratitude was given to American churches for their incalculable support and contributions, but not allegiance.

Keesee dealt with the issue by saying, "The Lord's work will continue in Nigeria. It has not been uprooted, as reported. We have some 55,000 brethren there who would keep the work going and cause it to grow if no American ever returned."[153]

To encourage the continuity of the work in Enugu areas, Keesee said that he left enough money with Brother Rufus Akitobi, a Nigerian preacher who worked with them in Enugu Bible College. The amount left to help support the Nigerian evangelists in the Enugu area would last for about four months. The *Herald of Truth* broadcast, originated via tapes from Enugu, will continue for about two months, even though they would not be there to pay the bills. It will likely terminate because no more tapes can be sent there until mail is resumed to Biafra.

The World Radio program, which was usually produced live, was discontinued. In a report to friends and some supporting churches, Keesee wrote, "Like the Ukpom work, it will be in the able hands of Brother Otoyo and other Nigerian brethren who taught in the Bible Training College. Dr. Farrar, the Gid Walters, the Gaston Targets, and the Wendell Keys are all still in the Aba area. Dr. Farrar is still seeing patients at the hospital, while Sister Farrar has the rest of the family with her at Lagos.[154]

The evangelistic work took different turns without American missionaries' physical presence. Many prayed, and words of encouragement helped to solidify the faith of the brethren at those virulent times. The church continued to march triumphantly, breaking barriers in the heat of the malaise that fractionalized families into different communities, where contact with one another was virtually impossible. God took care of us and the work.

Figure 24
L-R: Willie Cato, Houston Ezell, Bill Nicks

The measure of a person's greatness is not based on what he/she has kept but on what he/she has shared. Worldly gain and fortune are for a purpose; you do not give away without getting something in return. Houston and Mabel Zell gave what they had, but they also gave themselves and their family—children, sons-in-law, and grandchildren. They contributed at Vultee Church, where they worshipped, and at children's homes and numerous, worthy benevolent, nonprofit causes. With their practical hands-on Christian services, they raised people's dreams and hopes, they were encouragers.

Houston appeared on the Nigerian mission scene in the sixties as a member of the Board of Trustees of the Nigerian Christian Schools. He was likable, energetic, and by no means hesitant to meet people of different cultures. Race and color distinction were of no importance to him. He was one of the original members of the African Christian Schools and devoted his life to serving the cause of the kingdom. He visited Nigeria on numerous occasions in attempts to create a healthy educational environment for Nigerian children. He visited and taught in many congregations while pursuing the construction of buildings at Ukpom, Abak, and Oyubia Town, Oron.

As an entrepreneurial real estate developer and philanthropist, he invested his fortune freely to create a physically conducive educational environment for children. He made lasting impressions, not only by what he taught but because he perceived people as God's children. Houston Ezell was an accomplished builder who shared his construction skills with those who worked with him during the construction of the multipurpose building, which held a small library, classrooms, and a two hundred–seat assembly hall at the Nigerian Christian Secondary School at Ukpom, Abak.

At the Christian Technical College, Oyubia Town, Oron, he also came to Nigeria with his family, spending over a month in the construction of a 300 seat cafeteria, which later was converted into a temporary assembly hall; a business complex with five classrooms; and a domestic science demonstration bedroom and living room. This building was the initial capital investment that was donated by Brother Dean and Thelma Walling of Central Church of Christ in Los Angeles, California. At the same time, Ezell built the boys' dormitory simultaneously with the two other buildings, a feat that attracted the attention and curiosity of community members in the surrounding villages and Oron Town. People who visited the compound to witness the amazingly spectacular method of building so many buildings simultaneously were amazed.

Houston preached and taught in as many congregations as possible, but for him, the work was exciting and rewarding. Pioneers like Houston came only on brief trips, a few for an extended engagement. Common among them was that their eyes, hearts, and minds were focused on providing growth and stability to the work and people. Houston and his wife, Mabel, were irrefutable pioneers who served with calm and humility.

On December 7, 1959, Houston saw Jim Massey with his family arrive in Nigeria to serve in the Igbo areas as teacher at the Onicha Ngwa Bible Training School. Besides his regular assignment as a teacher at the school, Massey spent many days carrying a few sandwiches and a flask of water from dawn to dusk, while teaching in villages, persuading many to follow Christ. He was a prolific writer and publisher of numerous tracts that were distributed among the preachers and churches. Houston used some of Massey's tracts during his preaching appointments.

Joe and Dorothy Cross

Joe and Dorothy Cross, with their children, arrived Nigeria in June 1958 to serve their first term, primarily as the first administrator of the Nigerian Christian Secondary School at Ukpom, Abak. He arbitrated on disputes between the village and the school, which were frequent. He was a very patient man and sympathetic to the Nigerian cause. He regularly taught and preached at many churches in the villages, with many conversions.

Other luminaries who shone brightly as devoted ambassadors of Christ were people like Leonard Johnson, who served briefly as the manager of the elementary schools, and Douglas and Charla Lawyer, who came with their children and preached and taught at the Onicha Ngwa Bible School. Sewell and Caneta Hall, with their two children, Cherry and Gardner, were also in Nigeria. They toiled daily to prepare many young Nigerians for the ministry. Doug and Charla had a "home by the roadside," as we affectionately called it, that was a sanctuary for someone like me. They housed my wife and me after we had a serious car accident on the notorious Asaba Onitcha Road from Lagos. Joe and Dorothy were hospitable, accommodating the new missionaries who needed a place to stay or someone with whom to share their feelings of being in a strange land.

Chief Okon Effiong Mkpong

Figure 25
Proprietor of Nigerian Christian
Institute, Uyo, Akwa Ibom State

The impact of young and inexperienced ministers on the churches with young members, and in some cases, immature leaders compelled the missionaries and seasoned evangelists to look for and identify capable, mature, scripturally sound individuals to train and develop for leadership positions. Men and preachers with proven abilities to stabilize churches who would calm opposition and threats from gainsayers, were sought. Okon Mkpong was one among many who, after his conversion in 1956, proved to be an asset. He had an uncanny ability to challenge opposition without fear of reprisal. He was a courageous warrior of the gospel, a young man who openly spoke his mind, based on his knowledge, conviction, and understanding of the scriptures, whether one was a king, prince, or queen, and with respect and love.

Okon Mkpong attended the Government Primary, a nongovernment school, but later completed his primary education at St. Peter's Lutheran Primary School. In 1956, he attended the Nigerian Christian Bible College, Ukpom Abak, where his life changed drastically for the better. He also attended the Salvation Army Teachers Training College in 1961.

As was common in Nigeria for those who desired to advance their education professionally, he enrolled in the Wolsey Hall correspondence course in London, from which he qualified for the general education certification for grade 11 and the advanced GCE, including teacher grade 1, in 1970. With his wife, Affiong (Asuquo Bassey) Mkpong moved to Ukat Aran, where he taught and preached concurrently at the Christian School in Afaha Effiat and later served as the headmaster of Mbiabong Christian School.

In 1971, Brother Mkpong enrolled at Freed-Hardeman University, Henderson, Tennessee, and after earning his associate degree, he transferred to David Lipscomb University, Nashville, for his bachelor's degree. Later, he enrolled at Middle Tennessee State University for his master's degree in educational administration, graduating summa cum laude.

His emergence into the local political arena was, perhaps, not unusual but a deliberate reflection on his perception that the political system in Nigeria needed a change, no matter how minimal. He saw a perennially corrupt political system that thwarted progress, and he saw the longings of young people in the country. As in the 1950s and '60s in the United States, when church leaders vehemently censored or opposed Christians participating in elected political office, many Christians in Nigeria were vocal critics of the allegedly corrupt influence of politics.

Mkpong had made up his mind; he was convinced that Christians had the power to effect change and not always allow those who were perceived as evil politicians to enact laws that ultimately affected the poor and the powerless. In 1991, he ran for the coveted chairman position of Uyo Municipal Local Government Area. He won the election convincingly and was the first Church of Christ Christian who ever actively participated in politics, except Dr. Pullias of Pepperdine University,

Los Angeles, who contested and won the council seat. Mkpong was acclaimed as the most transparent politician in an era when political mismanagement, corruption, and favoritism was glaringly common and widespread.

More often, people are known not so much for what they verbalize but for their actions, which speak louder than words. As a Christian, he felt he must represent the values of honesty and fairness in dealing with people, especially with the large amount of money that was entrusted to his care for public use—and not for self-aggrandizement. On becoming the chairman of Uyo Municipal Administration, he said, "For the first time, I saw and was in control of large sums of money." As chairmen were privileged people who could use public money at their will to dignify themselves, he was also one among many who owned a Peugeot car, instead of other expensive cars. He never had an estate of luxurious buildings or houses in the housing estate, which was much like living in Beverly Hills, Los Angeles. Living in the estates at Uyo Nigeria was an opulent status symbol. He had to prove that a Christian could be involved in politics and remain a Christian, without tarnishing his image or dipping his hands in the cookie jar—he could be compelled by other power brokers without being tempted.

You cannot sublet your Christian beliefs and values. Okon Mkpong cited a statement he had once read: "If all were easy, if all were bright, where would the cross be, and where would the fight be? It is only in the hardness that God gives to your clearness of proving that you are true."[155]

He was appointed to the task force to recover public monies that were allegedly embezzled by political officials. So as not to patronize his clan yoke-men with contracts, an action that was tantamount to favoritism, he granted a contract to an Igbo contractor, for which he was reprimanded for having overlooked his people in the construction of Uyo local government offices.

Brother Ini Mkpong, his son, wrote that his father "entered politics because in our village, Afaha Udo Eyop, there was no medical [facility] or clinic. He wanted to help bring that and other development to the community. He completed the electrification of all forty-seven villages in Ibesikpo [and] other villages in Ikono as well as Afaha Udo Eyop, including a medical center."[156]

When the missionaries were forced to evacuate the country, Mkpong became the secretary of the board of trustees. The task of rebuilding and strengthening the churches was paramount for him. He was also appointed as the supervisor of the Church of Christ's eleven schools, while teaching at Ukpom Bible Training College. Brother Okon Mkpong was a man with an exemplary work ethic—a visionary, hardworking, diligent soldier of the cross. As of this writing, he continues to serve as the proprietor of the Nigerian Christian Institute, Uyo, Cross River State, Nigeria.

Figure 26
Ralph and Joyce Perry

Brother Ralph Perry was actively involved in the work in Warri. He focused his attention on the northern states in supervising the Bible school correspondence students. Perry responded to my questionnaire on October 13, 2016, saying, "Opportunities created through World B. School are tremendous. In 1980 there were no churches of Christ in Gongola state, but now there are nine and could be more if we could follow up properly. In Sokoto there was one church at Gusan [*sic*]. Now there are six churches in the state, and then added [strong Muslim ones]. There were twenty-five struggling churches in 1981 and these were made up of Southeasterners. There are over sixty with twenty to twenty-five members, made up of northern natives.[157]

Because of the scarcity of trained preachers, Perry encouraged eleven young men from the North to study at Ukpom Bible College. It was not unusual, but familiar situation that, if Muslim student converts, renounces or abnegate their Muslim religion for Christianity, and as though adding salt to injury, if recruited to attend the Bible school, once the parents know, family members automatically ostracize the student. Family vehement objection results in their rejection of the student regard him as a heathen and no longer as member of the family. The family refusal to support or help encourage the student to prepare for membership as preacher is another punitive method to force the student to recant. "Brother Perry and the college, in providing the Muslim students moral support, cooperatively raised support of fifty to sixty-five dollars for their schooling. [158] It is pertinent to mention that Brother Ralph Perry's path into Nigeria and the immense service in the World Bible correspondence program, including the effects of his follow-up program, particularly in the North, changed the religious terrain in some villages and towns in the Muslim North.

Initially, Ralph Perry and his family had a problem

entering Nigeria. As a direct consequence of the civil war, the federal government of Nigeria forbade the issuing of visas to missionaries from the United States. It was assumed that American missionaries covertly supported the enemy in the prosecution of the war, and only the British Commonwealth citizens had access to acquiring visas to enter Nigeria. When Brother Roger Church, one of the members of the African Christian Schools Board of Trustees, heard of the prohibition and the prospect that Ralph Perry, a Canadian and Commonwealth citizen, could enter Nigeria, Roger Church asked Ralph if he would consider a missionary trip to Nigeria.

At the time, Brother Ralph Perry was the chairman of Missions study group at Lipscomb College at Lipscomb, Texas. He was counseled that to enter the mission field, he must be married and have good health. From Lipscomb, he wrote, "I returned to Canada to prepare myself, waited for eighteen years, married, and had children before deciding to accept the challenge."[159]

The application process at the immigration office at Lagos was exasperating and frustrating. Some of the officers gave applicants the run-around. We were told, at one point, that Ralph noted, "Finally, I called the Nigerian High Commissioner's Office in Ottawa. That officer told me he knew my visa application was in Nigeria, and that they knew it was sent because it was sent by diplomatic bag. The officer then advised me not to take "no" for an answer, to insist that the application was indeed in Lagos."[160]

Following this instruction, in early 1971, I received the visas for Brother Perry and his wife. They arrived at Port Harcourt on April 7, 1971, where they met Brother Anako and LaVera Otoyo on the way from Ukpom.

From June 1980 to June 1995, Ralph Perry coordinated the World Bible School correspondence program follow-up in Nigeria. Later, Jimmy Lovell, the originator of the World Bible School correspondence program, persuaded him to do the WBS follow-up program, as there were more students in Nigeria than in any other country. Lovell warned him that the follow-up was the weakest aspect of the work.

Ralph Perry traveled to all parts of the northern states, resulting in a strategy he called the "four-ten plan," where experienced Nigerian preachers were sent to each of the northern states. They were not only to follow up but to evangelize and to start churches. As of April 23, 2003, there were over two hundred churches in the North and a Bible College in Jos, with Brother Solomon Agu as the director. With Steve Warley in Jos, Brother Perry returned to the Southeast to concentrate on the follow-up. In concluding his responses, he wrote these words of encouragement and inspiration:

I rejoice in knowing that thousands, yea, tens of thousands have accepted Christ as Savior, and hundreds of churches have been started through these efforts. World Bible School teachers have diligently done the teaching Nigerian preachers and church workers have followed up with further teaching and leading many to obey the gospel and start churches. I think of what Jesus said in gospel of John is true, that, 'Do you not say, there are yet four months more and then comes the harvest? I tell you, open your eyes and look at the fields! They are ripe for harvest. Even now the reaper draws his wages even now he harvests the crop for eternal life, so that the sewer (WBS teachers) and the reapers (WBS follow-up workers) may be glad (rejoice) together. Thus, the saying 'One sows, and another reaps' is true. "I sent you to reap what you have not worked for. Others have done the hard work, and you have reaped the benefits of their labor."[161]

The metaphor that Ralph paints was a recurring theme in many parts of the country as churches forged ahead, converting the unchurched. His work was not complete. He returned to Ukpom, where he recruited Dr. Timothy J. Akpakpan as an active Bible correspondence-student follow-up worker. Brother Henry Huffard and Steve Worley continued to coordinate the WBS follow-up.

Chief (Dr.) Moses Akpanudo

Figure 27
Chief (Dr.) Moses Akpanudo

The complexity of life and living is not always pleasurable, nor do people always achieve their goals, even with the best-laid plans. Perhaps Solomon, the wisest of them all, was right when he observed that in our dreams and achievements or even failures, "time and chance affects each of us I have seen something else under the sun: The race is not to the swift, or the battle to the strong, nor does food come to the wise or wealth to the brilliant or favor to the learned; but time and chance happen to them all."[162]

Every so often, events beyond our control abruptly shatter our dreams, and then, a window of opportunity may shine brightly. Moses Akpanudo learned about the Church of Christ during the Nigerian-Biafran War. He was a Mennonite preacher and the vice principal of Ibibio State College, Ikot Ekpene, Akwa Ibom State. During the war, Ibibio State College at Ikot Ekpene; Independence High School, Ukana, Ikot Ekpene; and St. Columbus Secondary School, Ikwem, were forced to merge as "refugee schools" to be accommodated at the Nigerian Christian Secondary's campus, Ukpom Abak. According to Akpanudo, Mr. Effiong U. Etuk was the overall principal of these three merged schools. It was here that Mr. Akpanudo was introduced to Mr. David Anako by a student who hailed from Utu Etim Ekpo, at Ukpom Bible School. David Anako, desirous of converting Akpanudo, gave him the book, *The Eternal Kingdom* by Dr. F. W. Mattox, the pioneer president of Lubbock Christian College, Lubbock, Texas. Studying the book, Akpanudo said that he realized for the first time that "there was a New Testament church."[163]

On January 15, 1970, he was converted. Immediately after the conversion, he returned to his village to teach his people his newfound religion, which was in opposition to the Mennonite teaching and doctrine. He organized and established the Christian Training Center for young men, and later, between 1971 and 1973, girls were added, culminating in a coeducational institution known as the Southern Annang Comprehensive Secondary School at Ikot Okoro, with him as the principal. Pleading for patronage, the African Christian Schools Foundation in Nashville, Tennessee, agreed to assist the people of that community in an attempt to develop the first comprehensive secondary school in the newly created Southeastern State.

Desiring to improve his academic competence, Akpanudo left for further studies in the United States in 1993. His wife, Jessie, joined him to pursue a degree in business economics at David Lipscomb College in Nashville, Tennessee, while Akpanudo enrolled at Peabody College. He was not content with seeking professional training; he sought other viable avenues where his community, the church, and the nation might be better served.

Upon his return to Nigeria, he established an educational ministry in Obong Ntak in 1977. In 1986, Obong Christian High School was started, including a nursery school. With all these schools, local evangelists and church leaders jointly established forty-three churches at Etim Ekpo, Ukanafun, and Oruk Anam Local Government Areas. A few years later, Akpanudo established the African College of Management in another part of the village. In 2007, the African College of Management gave way to Obong University, a school that has been described as the first degree-granting, privately run institution in the continent of Africa associated with the Churches of Christ.

His sterling record is exemplary, never deviating from his focus of bringing people to a true knowledge of God and Jesus as the Redeemer. He utilized the strategies of teaching, preaching, seminars, and workshops in the process of spreading the gospel.

Stephen Okoronkwo

Brother Stephen Okoronkwo was easily approachable, humorous, and entertaining. His outgoing character was an asset in his outreach ministry, as people gravitated toward him and listened to what he had to say. He was born at Obinkita in Arochuku, where the famous Long Juju cult was practiced. We never knew exactly why, in his early life, he never associated with others of his age in the cult.

Brother Okoronkwo had a somewhat radical mind; he never accepted or tolerated complex dogmas or view. He simply had difficulty discerning and sharing views that were relevant to the scheme of redemption. His parents, unlike other parents, may not have compelled him to attend church consistently. He, however, had basic knowledge and knew the principles of existing church doctrines. To know the difference in doctrine, he said he always compared what he knew with what he did not know and then made up his mind. This was the bridge he had to cross to accept the Church of Christ teachings, comparing his stock of previously learned information with the doctrine he later learned.

Okoronkwo was converted in the mid-1950s, when Brother Howard Horton, with his team, preached in one of the open-air gospel meetings. He told the story of meeting a "very tall American missionary" who was teaching. He attended the open lectures, not so much as to listen but to find fault or a window of opportunity to debate and argue.

Telling the story at Ukpom Bible College in his hilarious manner, he said that he was spellbound; he felt compelled, for the first time, to listen attentively to the contrasting issues that Horton discussed, to disprove the erroneous teachings and practices that existed in the denominational churches. Not fully convinced, he got the tracts that were offered. Later, he could not contain himself after a conscientious study of the tracts; he felt compelled to accept Christ as his Savior.

From this beginning, it was obvious he would be, not just a prospective student at the Bible Training School, but a leader and a bridge builder, using his linguistic abilities to bring people of different languages between the Igbos, Efik Ibibio, and English to Christ.

In 1955, Brother Okoronkwo enrolled at Ukpom Bible Training College for the two-year biblical studies. He had a great knack for amusing and entertaining, an attribute that endeared him to many. Soon after graduation, he moved to work with Brother J. W. Nicks, who was looking for a missionary post for settlement. He translated for many of the missionaries and taught at the Bible Training School, Onicha Ngwa, preaching, converting, and establishing churches and traveling extensively in many of the villages and towns—at Aba, Umuahia, Port Harcourt, Enugu, Abakiliki, Ikot Ekpene, Uyo, and beyond. It is difficult to enumerate the scope of Brother Okoronkwo's work or the extent to which he impacted the growth and stabilization of the work in Nigeria.

Brother Okoronkwo's advanced training in the United States at Oklahoma Christian College gave him the tools he needed for service. With his dear wife, Daphne, they were an unusual team in the programs they initiated. When the missionaries were finally forced to evacuate the country in 1967, Stephen and Daphne, LaVera Otoyo, Akandu, and a few other brethren were at Port Harcourt Airport with tearful eyes, weeping as the plane with the missionaries shot into the air. At the time, I observed the maneuverability of the plane, aloft high in the open sky, recalling Elishia in the Bible in his moment of exhalation and wonderment, expressing when Elijah, his mentor, vanished in thin air: "My father! My father! The chariots of Israel and the horsemen there off!"[164]

A few days earlier, the missionaries called a last-minute meeting to hand over the respective mission projects, buildings, and keys—like the keys of the kingdom to Peter in the Bible. Stephen Okoronkwo was an excellent team player. He, Josiah Akandu, and I first initiated the renewal of the annual land-lease contract of both the Nigerian Christian Hospital at Onicha Ngwa and the Bible Training School with Chief Ebere. Stephen was also deeply involved in the supervision of the Bible correspondence courses. He initiated a radio program at Aba, a program that became the mouthpiece for the church in reaching as many as could be reached.

The Nigerian-Biafran War was initially heralded with jubilation—women chanted songs of joy, and school children joined in without fully realizing the import, the consequences, or the impact of a civil war on people's welfare. It was just a euphoric sense for a political change at all costs. Nigerian men had experienced the First and Second World Wars; a few—just a few—died then, but never had Nigeria known or experienced the proportion of the conflagration of such an unpredictable time or the accompanying tragedies of the impending hunger and starvation of displaced people from their natural habitats.

In the affected areas, food was scarce, leaving those forced out of their habitats to scrounge for food and to live in makeshift tents or in orphan centers. The army that camped nearby, with security checkpoints, gave the college personnel a false sense of security. The danger did not come from the civil war but from a source one least expected. Onicha Ngwa, with its adjoining neighbor, had had scores of intermittent tribal conflicts for over fifty years. The presence of the police garrison, stationed to monitor and protect the war-mongering groups, was incapable of protecting the people because the groups exploited the blasé attitude of the police. One side would react violently when the other least expected, rampaging, destroying property in acts of vengeance, and killing whoever was in the way.

This time, the radicals from one side of the community took their vengeance out on the innocent personnel of Onicha Ngwa Christian School, including Brother Okoronkwo's beloved sister, Titi, whom they killed. They destroyed and stole all of Daphne's chickens, the only source of income, used to augment the little revenue they had during the war.

More hurtful than losing the farm was the loss of Stephen's sister, Titi, who was physically challenged, as she was mute. More than anything, that was a major precipitating factor that forced Stephen to evacuate the campus of a school he had sacrificed greatly to nurture.

The memory of the painful experience became a challenge for Steven not to give up. He relocated in Aba city, singlehandedly, with financial assistance from friends, to establish the Nigerian Christian Seminary, where many young men and women have been trained in survival skills and empowerment.

Figure 28
David Mbeke and Nelly Anako

One observed something very peculiar when meeting David Anako for the first time. He walked with broad shoulders, straight, with unflinching eyes fixed, as though reading through you. His gait was not swaggering but typical of a soldier, and indeed, he had been a soldier in the medical unit during the Second World War. His verbal account of how he became converted was through the help of a student of Ukpom Bible Training School, where he was introduced to a missionary at Ukpom.

Anako was previously a member of Qua Iboe Church, which was the dominant religious group in Etinan, Akwa Ibom State. When he enrolled at the Bible Training College in Ukpom in 1954, because of his stature, evident potential, and uncanny presence, he was made the supervisor of fellow students and later became an instructor at the school. Many of the succeeding missionaries depended on his wisdom and mature approach in social interactions with people; he became the counselor. Quite often, he interacted and intervened in conflicts between the community and school authorities.

He traveled and interpreted for missionaries, such as Howard Horton, Lucien Palmer, Joe Cross, and Glen Martin, who became the principal of Ukpom Bible Training College. He was a busy man who was involved with the Bible school, teaching and counseling, but he never forgot that his cherished responsibility was to actively preach. He established twenty congregations in areas like Akwa Ibom, Cross River, and Abia States. Brother Anako was responsible for and converted our beloved Dr. Moses Akpanudo, who later became an instructor at the Nigerian Christian Secondary School, Ukpom, Abak.

During the civil war years, Anako was a dependable

and indispensable ally to me. Upon the government edict, which forced all expatriates to depart Nigeria and the administrative control of the Church of Christ's establishments, Brother Anako was one of the most dependable persons to share in the supervision of the Bible school. A committee consisting of Brother (Chief) Okon Effiong Mkpong, Dr. Sunday Peter Ekanem, Brother Edet Essien, Josiah Akandu, Dr. Timothy J. Akpakpan, and Brother Stephen Okoronkwo were convened to determine an effective course of action for the management of existing religious and secular institutions of the church.

At this meeting, specific managerial responsibilities were delegated to Brother Anako, who assumed the role of principal of the Bible Training School. Okon Mkpong was responsible for the eleven elementary Christian schools. Edet Essien administered the Bible teachers, while Brother Josiah Akandu was made the acting administrator of the Onicha Ngwa Bible Training School, including the oversight of the properties of the compound; Stephen Okoronkwo served with Akandu.

With the delegation of responsibilities and roles, the burden was lifted from me, as I literally had been handed the keys of all the church establishments to oversee, a task only a person with Herculean ability could be proud to shoulder. I was by no means that, but I reluctantly accepted the challenge, believing there were many faithful, intelligent, and devoted soldiers to shoulder the duties and responsibilities of caring for the schools, including some preachers who depended on some missionaries for their livelihood.

The civil war that caused the disruption and dispersion of families, particularly those from the eastern Ibibio Ikono sector of the war, forced displaced people and members of the church to seek refuge in safe communities. Those who sought refuge were housed on the Bible Training School and the Nigerian Christian Secondary School campuses. Orphan home care, though available in some parts of the country, was still anathema in Nigeria. The preamble of the manual for the Children Care Center states that the developing child will reflect the treatment and training that is given. As an adult, his or her ability to find a place in society as a contributing member will either be strengthened or weakened by the experiences that he/she has had. It is, therefore, important that the responsibility for the care of each child be carefully always considered.

Through Quaker Service–Nigeria, Dr. (Mrs.) LaVera E. Otoyo's professional qualifications and experience in social work were unique, as she was consulted by the members of the Quaker Service committee to jointly develop the manual for the Children Care Center, a document that articulated which services would benefit displaced persons.

The manual was presented to the Southeastern State Ministry of Home Affairs and Social Welfare as a suggested guidebook for sponsors and administrators of full-time programs throughout the region. Brother Anako's role doubled as he was entrusted additionally with the managerial duties of the first orphanage of the Church of Christ. Two displaced children, ages seven and eleven, wandering and begging at Abak Town, were picked up and brought to Sister LaVera Otoyo, who, without prior knowledge or questions, agreed to care for them. The genesis of an orphan home could be attributed to the presence of these two—brother and sister.

Children Play House Church

Figure 29

These children led the establishment
of a new congregation.

Through these children, many other displaced members of Usuk Ukwok, Eastern Ibibio Ikono, bordering

Ibam Edet, who heard that the two children were at the Ukpom campus, joined them in search of refuge and food. Little did we know that these two children were God's little angels, and, as in Isaiah's statement, "The wolf will live with the lamb, the leopard will lie down with the goat, the calf and the lion and the yearning together, *and a little child will lead them*"[165]—that paradoxically would be true.

Immediately after the war, the brother and sister, with a few other refugees, returned home to start a church in an unbelievably small thatched "playhouse" structure they called a church. After they completed their playhouse church building, thirteen young people sent their representatives, traveling more than twenty miles to inform us that they had established a church (a group of young people with a building) and desired an appointment for us to preach to them.

There was no Church of Christ in the village. All they knew was what Brother Anako and others had taught them while they were refugees at Ukpom. The relationship and interaction with Christian influence had its impact. To them, establishing a church seemed like a way of showing gratitude, but their desired to share God's love with their communities was inherent and present.

Somehow, there were questions, one of which was whether the children's playhouse church would survive under the pressure of denominational churches that encircled them, whose members were older, mature, and stable. Among them, the oldest child was thirteen. We had no way to determine the survivability of the group as a church, except to pray with faith, hoping to identify an evangelist to minister to these children who were bound to be used as instruments to fulfill God's will.

And indeed, God did. From the chaos of the devastation, a mature evangelist was identified to provide the spiritual needs of the young congregation. With determination, persistence, and faith in God's guiding power, this congregation of seemingly immature young people grew to over two hundred members in twelve years.

About thirteen years later, two of the original children converts became preachers, and through them, four other churches have been established in the area. Their faith and hard work, influenced by the providential, powerful, guiding hands of God, shielded them from attacks.

Effiong John Ebong

Brother Effiong John Ebong, born to John Ebong and Jannie, of Ikot Obio Inyang in Etinan, was one of the most important leaders of the movement to introduce the church to many parts of Nigeria. He was indefatigable—a persevering soldier of the cross, who did not wait to act on the urging of Christ. Like many others, he was in the forefront of the battle to defend and proclaim the truth, regardless of circumstances.

Prior to becoming a member of the Church of Christ, he was a faithful member of the Qua Iboe Church. He was, in his own words, introduced by "a friend, a fellow teacher with me in the Qua Iboe Mission school, [who] told me about [C. A. O. Essien]; then I was moved to [visit] with him."[166]

Brother Ebong enrolled in the short-term three-month Bible course conducted by Brother C. A. O. Essien at Ikot Usen before attending the two-year Bible Training School at Ukpom, Abak. He was one of the initial eighty-four neophyte students who were curious and anxious, not knowing the scope or nature of the program, with no guarantees for financial remuneration to sustain them. God opened the door for the missionaries, like Howard Horton and Jimmy Johnson, who sought and got financial assistance for the students.

Initially, and as a prospective student, I had mixed concerns about the school, with its damp dormitory facility, which the community built to accommodate the students. The building was unappealing and unsuitable. When Brother Ebong, with Effiong Ating, heard I was considering withdrawing from the school, they persuaded me to remain. I respected the opinions and advice of these men and their unsolicited gesture of genuine concern for me.

After Brother Ebong graduated, along with forty-one others, from the rigorous two-year biblical studies, he intermittently taught and preached in as many congregations as possible. Brother Ebong, by nature, bore no grudges or ill will toward those with whom he disagreed, particularly on hermeneutical interpretation of the differences between theoretical understanding and practical application of the scriptures. In those areas of scriptural disagreement, he was firm yet loving, exhibiting gentleness and the trait of an uncommon bridge builder.

Ebong's energy and inclination, as he traveled for the cause of Christ, spanned many territories, as he systematically planted churches wherever he went. At some point, Wendell Broom, realizing Ebong's potential and ability, recommended Ebong, along with D. D. Isonguyo, Raphael Williams (currently known as Edet Eduok), and Solomon Etuk to Diestelkamp. Diestelkamp was, perhaps, instrumental in misguiding Ebong, who became a chief proponent of some adverse doctrinal issues, which tended to split the church, causing to impede evangelistic effort at Lagos.

They left for Lagos, where they met Brother Jacob Onobote, a barber by trade and already a Bible school correspondence student. Brother Onobote's barber shop was on Agarawu Street, in the heart of Lagos, where there was no church nearby. He had to travel to Ajegunle, where the church was first established, to worship. At the time, he said, "Brother Leslie Diestelkamp himself was living in Apapa, while I lived in Ajegunle," where the gospel was first received in Lagos State."[167]

On Lagos Island, the inhabitants were a tribally mixed community of Yorubas, Igbos, Ijaws, Efik Ibibios, and other groups. Ajegunle Church was meeting at No. 48 Orodu Street. He described this church as enjoying the first privilege because most of its inhabitants were Easterners, and all of us teamed up to work cooperatively. After three months, Brother Edet Eduok—later moved to worship with the Sixty-First Division Church of Christ in San Diego, California—moved to Surulere; Ebong relocated in Lagos Island; and D. D. Isonguyo remained at Ajegunle, where the church was already established. The church at Ajegunle was predominantly Yorubas, and the members spoke little, if any, pidgin (the adulterated) English. They sought a Yoruba-speaking preacher who could identify with and communicate in the Yoruba language, which would bridge the language problem.

With patience, they identified a minister for the church; they also secured a temporary meeting place at the New Age School building in 1959. In 1960, forging ahead, they established churches at Marako, Lagos Island, and Ikoyi, which merged with Lagos Island Church. Ebong wrote that "the last fruit of my labor was that of Apapa Road church, now meeting at Iponri village, while Brother Edet Eduok helped start the Surulere congregation. Since then, churches were established at Ebuta–Metta, Iwaya, Olodi, Agege, Mushin, Oshodi, Ikeja, Shomolu, and Palm Grove."[168] Brother Ebong then listed eleven American missionaries who arrived to enhance the spreading of the Word and establish churches.

Ebong was instrumental in publishing subsequent Christian hymn books, which originally were compiled, edited, and published by Brother Essien Ekanem of Ntan Ekere. Ebong published some tracts and established the six-month Bible school at Paul Bassey Street, the brainchild of his dreams, where many aspiring preachers and church leaders attended to improve their knowledge of the scriptures.

The program, which became a break–away group with slight changes in doctrine, was ill conceived. Many became "experts" in their interpretation of passages that they viewed as contradicting what the main group Church of Christ (the liberals) believed and practiced. What became clear was that those who graduated from the six-month biblical program had the zeal but not full knowledge of the scriptures. They parroted information they received. Regardless, Brother Ebong was unique. He was either establishing churches or assisting aspiring committed Christians to venture into unknown territories.

Figure 30
George U. Ekong

Brother George U. Ekong was born at Nung Ukot in Itam and learned the skill of iron tinkering, otherwise called iron fabrication, professionally. He took residence at Iwok No. 1, where he practiced his profession, which enabled him to preach without having to depend on churches that were young and incapable of financially supporting an evangelist. Brother Ekong was baptized on July 15, 1954, and soon thereafter, he was taught by Brother C. A. O. Essien in one of the three-month Bible courses at Ikot Usen, Ibiono Ibom, in Itu Local Government Area and then Southeastern State. He wrote that his teachers were C. A. O. Essien, Howard P. Horton, Eugene Peden, Elvis Huffard, and Lucien Palmer.

Brother Ekong was a devoted family man who cared enormously about his children and believed strongly in the importance, the influence, and effects of Christian education. He therefore encouraged his children to attend any of the existing Christian institutions, from which five of them graduated before their advanced college training. He exhibited a deep sense of humility, honesty, fairness, and responsibility—characteristics needed to be successful in a people-oriented profession. When he became an evangelist, these attributes spilled over into his service among the churches that he established.

During the civil war, Brother Ekong was one of the members of the food-distribution team, with materials donated by the Lagos group of churches, on which Brothers Effiong John Ebong, Essien Ekanem, and D. D. Isonguyo served as overseers and distributors. Brother Ekong mentioned that Ufot Jacob also participated in the food distribution. In 1954, he traveled extensively with Brother Nelson Isonguyo, visiting churches at Oyubia Oron; Mbokpu Eyoakan; Udung Uko (one of the fishing villages in Oron); Oruko; and Oron Town for Bible classes. When Brother Isonguyo left for advance studies in the United States, he took over the full-time care of the few churches established in Oron because there were preachers working in Oron.

The only available preachers in Oron were Edet Ononokpono and Effiong Okon Umoh, who served in other areas. He reported that he cooperatively partnered with Brother Effiong Atte Enyenihi at Ikot Abasi Asutan, while Etim Robert Offiong preached at Idoro Central Church in Ibiono Ibom, Itu, Akwa Ibom State.

Later, Brothers S. U. Nsek and S. O. Ambia returned from Calabar, and Brother Ekong said that they cooperatively forged ahead on the expansion of the church. Consequently, churches were growing by leaps and bounds; converts were registered in surrounding villages. When F. F. Carson and Levi Kennedy visited Nigeria, they baptized sixty-eight in the first congregation they attended. At Ibiakpan Nsit, sixty souls were converted; at Osu Ofi, ten souls were converted; at Afaha Nsung in Okobo, seven were baptized; and at Okopedi, five people were converted.

Ekong could not to be stopped in his zeal and determination to see that churches were established in as many localities as possible. In Eastern Nsit, he established the following churches, aided by a few other individuals who accompanied him: Ikot Inyang Nsit (1956), Ikot Akpanike Nsit (1956), Ibedu Nsit (1954), Ikot Ubok Udom (1965), Ikot Abia Enyie (1967), Iwok Nsit (1970) with Udo Nkono, Ikot Obon Nsit (1972), Akpan Offep (1973), Idiaba Nsit (1973), and Ndon Ekpe (1974.)

Brother Ekong could be viewed as a man unchained and unwilling to allow any distraction or human impediments to deter him from proclaiming the redemptive message of God's Son. In Oron clan, with a small band of preachers, small congregations were established between 1975 and 1978 at Otieke Offi, Osu Offi, Utine Nduong, Ebihi Anwa, Ikpe, and Mbokpu Oduobo. Oron Town Church dispersed and no longer met during Brother Walter Umoh's tenure as the preacher of that congregation.

In 1966, the following preachers jointly converged in Oron Town: G. U. Ekong, S. U. Nsek, Felix J Bassey, S. J. Ambia, and Okon from Duomo in Ubiom, in a daring effort to restore the church at Oron Town. Brother Ekong was indeed the embodiment of a true servant of the Lord as he ventured into unknown territories in Oron.

In 1965, Brother Ekong established the church at Nsie and Eweme, Oron. In 1957, traveling with Brother Philip Inua, Effiong Ating, they established churches at Otieke Offi, Osu Offi, Utene Nduong, and Ebighi Anwa Ikpi. In 1968, others joined George Ekong and established the church at Mbokpu Oduobo. As he continued to reach more people, he and a few spiritual colleagues moved to Ubiom, where they established the following churches: Akai Ubiom (1966), Ikot Eyo (1968), Ntiti Oton (1967), Ndukpo Ise (1979), and Ibono in Eket (1964.) Between 1964 and 1972, the following churches were established: Afaha Nsung and Okopedi, Oron Road Church.

Brother Ekong reported that the total number of churches established was twenty-five; then he listed, in collaboration with other writers, the names of preachers who worked before the coming of the American missionaries in 1948. The missionaries he listed were Howard P. Horton, 1952 to July 1954; Jimmy Johnson, 1952 to July 1954; Eugene Peden in 1953; and Elvis Huffard from December 4, 1953 to April 16, 1955.[169]

Ekong listed the names of expatriate missionaries that were in Nigeria between 1956 and 1966 and at the onset of the civil war in 1966. Ekong reported that the evaluation of missionaries was a precautionary measure against reprisals, for fear they might be physically harmed. Brother Burney Bawcom devoted his energy to teaching and preaching against the evils and the demoralizing effects of polygamy. Wendell Broom, who also taught at the Ukpom Bible Training College, envisioned the concept of developing a dialogue among African churches and encouraging indigenous self-supporting churches in Africa. In Broom's document, he listed the following missionaries who quartered at Ukpom Abak at different times: Miss June Hobbs, Billy Nicks, Leonard Johnson, Sewell Hall, James Finney, Tommy Kelton, Rees Bryant, Joe Cross (who served as the first principal of the Nigerian Christian Secondary School, Ukpom, Abak), Glenn Martin, and Cathy Newberry.

James Massey, Jim Sasser, and Douglas Lawyer, with no orientation except what Jim Massey and Rees Bryant provided him, went from village to village, teaching and preaching. Iris Hays and Nancy Petty (both have since married) were the first two missionary women at the Nigerian Christian Hospital at Onicha Ngwa. Without exception, these men and women provided the impetus and the direction for the growth of young churches in Nigeria. Their lives were a monument in the annals of the history of the growth of the Church of Christ in Nigeria.

Solomon U. U. Etuk

Solomon U. U. Etuk was a good friend and a partner in tribulation among the skeptics within hard-core denominational leaders in the then-Itu district. After graduating from Ukpom Bible Training School in 1955, both of us were assigned to preach; he headquartered at Ntan Ekere, while I was stationed at Mbiatok, Itam. Both of us shared equally more than fifty-four churches. It was a seemingly impossible task to meet the spiritual needs of these congregations, visiting and establishing churches, with the aid of our bicycles, in villages where the church was never started or heard.

Solomon was a good soldier of the cross— unpretentious, devoted to the cause, always willing to share from his lean means with some of the members he served. Solomon, like most of the young graduate preachers, earned seven sterling pounds per month, an amount, though grossly inadequate, that was appreciated and that enabled him to do full-time work. Often, he would use a portion of his income to purchase Communion wine for some of the congregations that were new and without money to even feed themselves. These were hard times for most of our preachers. Solomon was well versed in the scriptures and was always ready to debate or share his knowledge and love of scriptures at any time. He was indeed a dependable soldier of the cross.

Figure 31
Carroll and Bernice Pitts

Brother Carroll Pitts was one of nine children born to Carroll and Algertha Pitts in North Little Rock, Arkansas. He was converted by Henry Clay Tyner in 1944 and was married to Bernice M. Carr in Los Angeles, California. He attended Booker T. Washington High School in Tulsa, Oklahoma, and later attended Pepperdine University, where he earned a bachelor's degree in religion, and a general teaching credential at California State University, Fresno. He returned to Pepperdine University, where he earned his master's degree in religion.

Carroll Pitts conducted numerous gospel meetings, workshops, seminars, and lectures in twenty-three states. In 1962, sixteen years after Marshall Keeble and Lucien Palmer's visit to Nigeria, Carroll Pitts's evangelistic visit, with a group of twelve, was initiated. Carroll Pitts was better known as an Afro-American minister with a nonmilitant reputation, particularly on racial issues, but he did not take a docile or compliant position. Though appearing to be moderate, he was firm, not dodging the irrational racial bigotry that was common among most of the white churches, as well as Christian colleges and universities. He already had led mission campaigns to Guyana, South America; Kingston, Jamaica; the Bahamas; and New Zealand. He taught religion classes part-time at Pepperdine University for approximately nine years. He also made five trips to the Holy Land as a tour guide. At this point, one would say he was ready to enter Nigeria, a new phase of a global mission, with a focus on an enduring evangelistic ministry.

In 1980, Carroll Pitts jointly cosponsored a team of

successful church leaders and ministers on a two-week tour to Nigeria. Carroll knew that traveling to Nigeria was not easy or straightforward. There were preparations, challenges, and passport and visa acquisitions, and once there, the living environment was not pleasant. While other missionaries were tentative about socializing with the villagers and members, Carroll blended easily with the community, churches, and students, as though he was no stranger.

The missionary trip groups that he guided to Nigeria were divided into four zones: (1) Lagos, (2) Calabar, (3) Oron, (4) Abak and Uyo. Each zone had a local leader, who planned outreach teaching and preaching among the respective communities. At Aba, a congested commercial center with many churches already established, there existed the Bible Training School and the Nigerian Christian Hospital, eleven miles away from Aba. Brother Stephen Okoronkwo was the facilitator of the group, which was composed of Brother and Sister William Harper and Brother Jimmy E. Johnson, one of the first missionaries to Nigeria in 1952. Brother Johnson, understandably, desired to spend his time with the churches in Itu communities, where he'd first lived, worked, and established many churches.

The Lagos zone was facilitated by Brother Etim Asuquo, who was assigned Brother Howard Ewing, known as the "Lone Ranger" because he was the only one without a visiting partner. At Uyo, the capital city of Akwa Ibom State, Brother Okon Mkpong was the facilitator, and Elvis Huffard was a former missionary to Nigeria, the director of Christian Counseling Services in Florence, Alabama, and dean of Student Affairs at Henderson. Other members of the group were Burney Bawcom; Sister Bernice Pitts; Harvey Johnson, an elder at Avalon Church of Christ, Los Angeles; and Sister Alice Fisher, a member at the Normandie Church of Christ in Los Angeles. These brethren were committed and tireless. They traveled from community to community, and they exemplified the spirit of true servants of God. In every area, they observed the overwhelming nature of the work, the potential, and the opportunities to share Christ among people who were eagerly receptive to the message. At the end of the two weeks, they had converted thirty-eight people; eighteen of these were at the Christian Secondary Technical School campus, Oyubia, Oron, where Brother Pitts taught daily.

Peter Akwaowo

Brother Peter Akwaowo was the missionaries' consummate professional mechanic and driver. As a mechanic, he repaired all the missionaries' cars, both at the Ukpom and Onicha Ngwa compounds. He kept the missionaries moving and responded to the medical emergency needs of community members who needed transportation to hospitals.

When the missionaries evacuated the country due to the civil unrest, he was without a job or source of income. Money was no longer forthcoming from America; food and necessities were suddenly interrupted. Black-market trading soared; prices skyrocketed to the extent that many could no longer afford to sustain themselves.

Brother Akwaowo was resourceful, though not an entrepreneur by any means. He resorted to trading— buying crawfish and fish from Oron, Itu, and Opobo beaches, where he purchased these items at wholesale for retail distribution. From a minimal financial investment, he derived extraordinarily little profit, but it was enough to take care of some of the family's basic needs.

Brother Akwaowo was never involved actively in the civil war, but he witnessed hundreds of Nigerian soldiers as they marched down the road where he and his family lived. One can never predict the circumstances of one's demise, especially where maximum care must be exercised in handling gasoline. He simply miscalculated the explosive power of gasoline as he prepared to drive to Ikot Abasi to purchase goods.

Early in the morning, he was siphoning gasoline from another car into his station wagon, using a bush lantern for light. He assumed he had placed the bush lantern at a safe distance. Suddenly, he was engulfed in the explosive torch of gasoline. Both Brother Akwaowo and the car were instantly engulfed in flames. He died four days later at Ikot Okoro Lutheran Hospital. His loss was keenly felt by his family—his wife and three children, the extended relatives, missionaries, and friends he knew and served. His death was catastrophic to the village, the school, and the missionaries, who depended on him for their daily transportation.

CHAPTER 7

Rehabilitation Effort during the Civil War

War between tribes and nations is disruptive. It is a chaotic, despicable evil. It affects the physical, psychological, and spiritual makeup of individuals. Parents, children, and other family members are caught in the middle, forced to evacuate and relocate in unfamiliar territories, where food, shelter, clothing, and other necessities are unavailable to sustain body and spirit. Children, who are usually most affected, are confronted with physical harm, violence, and vicious emotional and image-shattering experiences.

The Nigerian-Biafran War, from 1966 to '69, affected human lives by the destruction of property, displacement of families, and the killing of innocent children and men, assumed to be in the way of the combatants. The atrocities against Biafra's ethnic minorities included clans like Efik, Calabar, Ibibio, Oron, and Ikot Abasi. Robert Melson recorded the inhumanity and mercilessness of the warring groups as monstrous. In 1966, he wrote, "I was in my late twenties, thousands of Ibos (Igbos) were massacred in Northern Nigeria. Later in 1967 leading until 1970, one million, perhaps as many as two million people starved to death."

Robert Melson thought that, should Biafra fail, Ibos would be massacred by the Nigerian soldiers. Thankfully, he and others who thought this way, eventually felt they were wrong. Nigerians were not Nazis, and the Ibos were not Jews even though some of them feel proud to accept this characterization. General Gowon, the army ruler, was sympathetic in his own way. He protected the Ibos and would not permit the extermination of Igbos because of the relationship with his wife, who was Igbo from the East.

Unfortunately, with some of his field officers, this was not so. The notorious Colonel Benjamin Adekunle, who was described as a notoriously gruesome commander of the Nigerian army, boasted, without qualms, about his horrendous mission goal to exterminate Biafra. Adekunle carried out a personal vendetta with surgical precision, especially targeting Southern Igboland. He slaughtered hundreds and thousands; he boasted of destroying anything that moved in Biafra.

Accurate statistical records in Nigeria are a joke. Every census for the last twenty years or more has been controversial and a subject of argument. The statistics on number of deaths during the civil war have not been ascertained. No one really knows how many soldiers— both from Nigeria and Biafra—and children lost lives, resulting from the civil war. There are no records, since no records were kept on the number of children or adult civilians who died of starvation or malnutrition. The nation has no verifiable statistics of its people, and what one hears is always an acrimonious and vehemently contested record.

What is known and accepted are the numbers that the Nigerian government provided, which were exaggerated for public or international consumption. The British Mission reported in 1968 that 200,000 people were estimated to have died every day. Two months later, the International Committee of the Red Cross estimated eight thousand to ten thousand deaths per day. The record was based on barometric accounts of deaths in villages, refugee camps, and hospitals. Jean Mayer, professor of nutrition from Harvard School of Public Health, estimated that the ten thousand deaths a day appeared accurate.

As an eyewitness during the war, especially in Akwa Ibom State, I observed the height of inhumanity in the cities of Uyo, Ikot Ekpene, Abak, Oron, and Ikot Abasi, where hundreds and thousands of abandoned children suffered from starvation and the ill health of kwashiorkor (protein malnutrition) and died. At the school where I lived, battalions of soldiers marched down the only bush path in the area, allegedly to prosecute the war but traversing to their doom, never to return.

A soldier in the battalion, who must have known about my wife's chicken farm, broke formation, walked directly to the chicken farm, took one of the chickens, and then returned to his rank with the chicken. My wife ran after the soldier to recoup her chicken. Roars of laughter erupted, mostly among the soldiers, who could not resist laughing over the struggle for the chicken between the soldier and Mrs. Otoyo. She, without fear of being shot, bravely recovered her chicken. Perhaps this was the last great laughter the soldiers had as they marched to their final destiny. They never returned.

My younger brother, Effiong Otoyo, who was in the Nigerian army, had come late in the evening, two days prior, to inform us that the Nigerian army was in the bushes, ready to comb the surrounding bushes, beginning at 9:00 p.m. And indeed, by 9:00 p.m., we heard the frightening rattling and intermittent clattering of gunshots in the bushes surrounding our home. Two weeks later, one of the surviving soldiers returned to bring the bitter news that our brother Effiong Caesar Otoyo had been killed in the encounter to capture Port Harcourt.

In many towns, cities, and villages, homes were recklessly burned, and men were shot as revenge. At Abak and particularly the Ikot Ekpene police station, dead bodies were strewn around a courtyard the size of a soccer field. Some had been killed; others died of starvation. Many lay in the mercilessly hot tropical sun, barely alive, panting for breath. People with shrunken bodies, like dried leaves, wheezed and gasped for breath as they lay on the ground, waiting to die.

These were images reminiscent of forced conditions, where men's evil doings created hardship for innocent people. The trauma faced by displaced persons, especially when they experienced torture, rape, and beatings, are memories they carried with them as they wandered and scavenged for food. No wonder many felt helpless and afraid, as victims in strange and inhospitable communities.

Remedial rehabilitation in the war-torn areas was crucially and urgently needed. With a little local assistance and help from the United States, a committee was set up in 1966 to oversee and supervise the distribution of assistance to preachers and local congregations and in places where families were displaced. The brethren at the Una congregation in Nashville, Tennessee, under the leadership of J. P. Neal, acting on behalf of the elders, contributed to the support of preachers.

On June 9, 1976, in the minutes/record of the committee meeting held on the campus of the Bible college, Ukpom Abak, Brother Effiong O. Mkpong summarized the purpose of the meeting, wondering what form of relief activities to the areas worst hit by the Nigerian Civil War we should take.

The members of the committee, composed of Brothers Edet Essien, Sunday P. Ekanem, David M. Anako, and I, were without the financial capability to handle the needs. However, we shared the desire and longing to do whatever was possible under the circumstances. On my recommendation, as chairman of the Relief Committee, a special committee was formed to study the available information to ascertain the true situation in these areas and how funds from the brotherhood might be raised and distributed.

S. P. Ekanem, David Anako, Edet Essien, and Okon Udo (Chief), in their respective teams, conducted a week's survey of the churches that were severely affected by the war. The data gathered during this period reflected the following results, which were published in the following analysis of the events as they occurred between 1967 and '69:

Divisions/Areas	Homes Destroyed	Church Buildings Destroyed	Deaths
Ibiono	400	13	170
Abak	364	17	1010
Eastern Ibibio Ikono	361	13	258
Ikot Ekpene	214	19	198
Calabar	164	4	49
Eket	54	4	71
Opobo (Ikot Abasi)	26	10	80
Itam	47	1	108
Uyo	44	1	354
Total	1,674	82	2,298

These statistics were gathered by the different members of the rehabilitation team, a collaborative effort of the Churches of Christ.

Through the reports given by surveyors and members of the committee who visited the respective areas, it was noted that food scarcity was alarming in most areas. The people of Ibiono and parts of Abak Division, Eastern Ibibio Ikono, and Ikot Ekpene were saved from starvation through the food supplies given by the officials of the National Rehabilitation Committee. Malnutrition was rampant in these areas, and medical facilities were inadequate. Mobility was greatly hampered. The people, including many of the preachers, sold their bicycles in the early period of the conflict to enable them to survive. Those who still had bicycles could not afford to repair and keep them on the road. People walked miles to food distribution centers; an example of this was Brother Akpan Dickson, who traveled thirty miles from his home, through Ikot Ekpene, to meet the brethren for his needs.

Committee Recommendations

1. Homes: It was roughly estimated that materials needed for building a temporary home for a family of four would cost twenty sterling pounds, on average. After a lengthy discussion on how the relief committee should help Christians

and, where possible, the general public in these communities to start buying building materials, it was recommended that each of the families be given ten sterling pounds.

2. Church buildings: It was observed that in nearly all the areas concerned, building materials were very scarce because of the incessant bombings. To erect a temporary meeting place, which would accommodate an average of two hundred members, the materials would cost at least thirty sterling pounds. The committee, therefore, recommended that each of the congregations so affected be given twenty sterling pounds initially to help the members start buying building materials. Meanwhile, it was recommended further that five sterling pounds be shared among the congregations.

3. Victims: To help the victims in the areas so badly affected, it was recommended that each member of the committee be given a minimum of fifty sterling pounds, cash, to carry along for emergency distribution to individuals in the affected communities.

4. Medical supplies: The committee noted that the coming of Dr. Henry Farrar was a God-sent blessing that would do quite a lot to help alleviate the unimaginable hardships in those parts due to

vitamin and protein deficiency in their meals. It was hoped that during the moment of emergency, Henry Farrar's field work would be expanded to cover war-torn parts of the East Central, South Eastern, and Rivers States. Members expressed thanks to God for Dr. Farrar and the brethren in America who made his coming possible. It was believed that when he returned from the United States on his trip, he would make arrangements to remain in Nigeria permanently with his team. It was hoped that the brethren would give him sufficient equipment to help meet the challenges of his medical mission.

5. Igbo in Southeastern State: Mr. Sunday P. Ekanem [the secretary] recommended that in parts of Ini Development Council area, Igbos living in Okolomakri communities be given the sum of 168 sterling pounds still left from other Igbo relief centers.

Conclusion: The report is the result of a survey made by a team of seventeen faithful preachers and teachers. This team, in their respectively assigned divisions, visited 380 churches and talked to over two thousand persons, both members of the church and nonmembers.

To ascertain the scope of needs in specific areas where relief activities should be effected, we were forced to delay active relief temporarily. We discovered that certain areas were less affected, and therefore, little assistance was needed in those areas. The views on this seemed to be unanimous, even though it was generally agreed that areas less hard-hit suffered from looting and still had need for some assistance.

We therefore need and appeal for intensive and consistent relief for the following divisions for approximately six to nine months:

1. Ibiono and Itu
2. Abak, Aka clan
3. Eastern Ibibio Ikono
4. Ikot Ekpene

The above areas lost land and crops; it will take years to recover their homes and property.

May we point out that the survey, apart from discovering the needs of the people, observed that there were more than 380 churches in the South Eastern State of Nigeria; 2,498 members of these churches were either killed as a direct result of the war or died from natural causes during the war.

Regrettably, this survey was not carried out in Igbo areas; we would, however, point out that great relief is needed, and like the four divisions cited above, certain areas in Igboland should be on the priority list.

One of the greatest difficulties or handicaps was transportation. Most team members of the Church of

Christ relief operation used bicycles, which made it difficult, if not impossible, to reach many. We were limited in our relief efforts and strongly appeal to our brethren to consider a truck, which will enable us carry out effective relief work and help facilitate easy transportation and the distribution of foodstuffs and other humanitarian supplies.

The committee suggested that approximately eight thousand sterling pounds each month for nine months should be considered for the areas specified.

> E. Otoyo, Chairman
> Presented by O. E. Mkpong, Secretary.
> Church of Christ Relief Team
> PO Box 137, Uyo
> South Eastern State of Nigeria

The destruction of properties, the heavy loss of human lives, the dispersion of people from their natural homes, and the uncertainty of their daily bread left many in a broken emotional state but did not break their faith. Many were served, and their needs were met.

The rehabilitation during the civil war produced men of valor who were capable, ready, and willing to respond to the gospel call. The era of church growth did not end in the year 2000. It was simply an arbitrary, convenient period in which this narrative ended. Church growth never ends with single individuals. The church, as an organism, with the right doctrines and Christian-based practices, continues to grow, but its abilities must be tested and respond in time of acute national need.

The period of the Nigerian–Biafran War, 1966–1969, also covered the flight and dispersion of inhabitants from their homes; this gave Christians, who never had engaged in a large-scale rehabilitation effort, things to ponder. They developed a rehabilitation-organization structure in consideration of issues like food, first aid, medical needs, clothing, shelter for those whose homes were demolished, and, in some cases, a minimal stipend. All of these were instructive and encouraging for them to reflect. They could not become complacent or rest on the little they had accomplished, but they gave God, who shows mercy to the poor and helpless, the glory.

CHAPTER 8

Challenge to the Faith (The Anti-movement)

The purity and doctrine of the church has caused schisms and unhealthy rivalries among the brotherhood for centuries. In the first century, from AD 33, Paul the apostle wrote extensively on numerous issues, such as schisms and that some held themselves as better than others. The church also faced sexual immorality, idolatry, and division. Over the years, the difference in doctrinal teachings and practices often has resulted in the splintering of churches into factious groups.

Paul's apologetic narrative to the Corinthian church dealt with some of these issues. In the first century, early disciples used existing temples and synagogues as worship places until Jewish leaders opposed Gentiles' admission into the church, where some Jewish members held the strict, dogmatic view that for Gentiles to be granted membership in the church, they must be Jewish proselytes.

Marcionism rejected the commandments of Christ; the Gnostics were the religious rationalists who, through their own mental gymnastics, solved problems that reflected their own speculative philosophical views. Mattox, on the other hand, pointed out that the Docetists believed and taught that Christ did not really suffer. Other varying views that deviated from what the scriptures teach held doctrines that could be equated to the modern anti-movement follower's perception. In a letter to Roger Church, dated November 26, 1971, Brother J. W. Nicks showed the problem that the anti-movement brethren posed. At the conclusion of his visit to Lagos, Brother Nicks wrote,

> "I have been in Lagos for a week helping Brother Thomas battle the anti- problem. I have had two lectures each day at two different Lagos churches, each lasting two hours or more. Diestelkamp has printed and sent several thousand tracts answering Jim Massey's charts and they feel the force of our teaching. They had full sway during the war and gained headway with no one to check them, but we are getting across to many that *they are the ones sewing discord* [emphasis added]. Paul Bernhardt showed up at one of my lectures. He has just come in for 'few weeks' and he is concerned about the trouble in the churches and has come on a mission of peace, but of course, like Communism, they want peace on their terms.[170]

Paul's opposition to the faction that arose at Corinth was a result of individuals and groups that advocated unscriptural doctrines or imposed on scripturally unlearned, innocent followers' unscriptural views and practices. Unfortunately, the Nigerian anti or conservative members appeared to know extraordinarily little about the origins and rise of their own movement.

Brother Daniel Sommers, a leading member of the group, took a radical extremism approach to issues that splintered the church. After building a significant membership from Pennsylvania to Colorado, he fought the progressives, who, at the time, had become the Christian Church. He attacked anyone among the brethren who did not adhere to his dictates. Though there were moderate voices, like David Lipscomb, Sommers's attitude plagued the church in a way that their influence reverberated, perhaps unknowingly, among the Nigerian anti-movement brethren.

The influence and teachings of Sommers did not die with him in 1940. His cohorts and followers, like Fanny Yater Tant and Roy Cogdill, who wrote the booklet, "Bible Topics" with Foy Wallace, championed the launching of the non-institution movement in 1947–49. The non-institution movement consisted of the splintered Christians of the Church of Christ, who advocated noncooperation in the areas described in the paragraph below.

After a few months, Tant and Cogdill clashed with Wallace, who separated himself from the others. After a short period, Wallace reappeared, announcing that both Tant and Cogdill were divisive and wrong. Because of the anti-movement and spirit, no persuasion could keep the two groups together as a unit. The leaders of the mainstream church, like Guy N. Woods, B. C. Goodpasture, G. K. Wallace, Thomas Warren, and Roy Deaver, who were notable pillars of the church at the time, produced the principal journal in lessons that exposed the weaknesses and errors of the objectors.

In 1960, division among the groups became a reality. The anti-movement, according to John Walden, gradually added other binding issues to the list of forbidden practices, such as "eating in church building, sending funds to a missionary via an overseeing [eldership]."[171]

As it was in the United States, so it became in Nigeria that the anti-movement brethren, led by Diestelkamp and his bedfellows, continued to rail at the mainstream preachers and churches. A radical preacher of the group opposed local preachers, orphan homes, and Christian schools. Before discussing the issue with the board of trustees, as required by the government, here are the issues alluded to:

1. The anti-movement falsely accuse missionary supporters of being untrue to Christ.

2. They seek to impose man-made rules and restrictions on the brotherhood.

3. Christians (the church) cannot support or establish and administer a school or an orphan home to care for abandoned, displaced children.

4. Christians, like their predecessors, cannot provide benevolence to nonmembers or establish a hospital to care for the sick.

5. Churches cannot cooperate in evangelistic outreach activities.

6. Christians cannot enjoy a fellowship in their existing place—the church building.

7. The elders of one congregation cannot handle the funds (of the church) contributed by others for a missionary service abroad.

8. The World Bible School (WBS), which has converted thousands, is unscriptural.

One of the issues that faced Nigeria concerned the board of trustees, a legal instrument promulgated by the government for any person or organization desiring a legal presence within the country to perform specific purposes. Usually, the nonprofit organization would articulate their purposes to align with what the government prescribed as the purposes, which were not of a subversive political nature.

When the first missionaries of the Church of Christ arrived in the country, they could not operate legally without registering. This did not preclude, however, any autonomous church or individual from registering as an independent church to perform whatever religious, benevolent, educational, or social services they desired to perform. The anti-movement group knew or perhaps were ignorant of this position, but they still depended on the mainstream group to function. The registration stated their aims, as prescribed, or provided by the federal government, with the membership of this corporation to constitute three officiating members: the chairman, the secretary, and the treasurer. The incorporation of the board of trustees was exclusively to facilitate the entry of missionaries who shared the same beliefs and practices in their ministry and never included any person whose views and doctrinal teachings were antithetic, detrimental, or in opposition to what the mainstream advocated.

Many failed to realize, however, that to have permitted any person to come under the umbrella of the registered trustee who represented missionaries, sharing similar views and practices, was as hypocritical as it was dishonest. The question would be, "How does a person knowingly grant sanctuary in his house to a friend, if, in fact, he is a friend who would betray him when he is away, leaving his wife alone in the house?" And again, does one give a dagger to someone who would discredit him, cause division, and teach unscriptural doctrine against him?

What we feared and could not provide—the approval of Leslie Diestelkamp—prophetically came to pass, causing division and intemperate rhetoric within the flock. The board of trustees established by the mainstream Church of Christ in Nigeria never dictated any law to govern an autonomous congregation. They operated purposely for the sole interest of recruiting missionaries whose teachings and doctrines were in alignment with that group. However, any congregation that choose to function under the conditions as explicated by the federal government could so join and function, but *not the church*.

The anti-movement brethren failed to understand or accept their legal limitations. Even with all this contention and squabbling on doctrinal issues, the church continued to grow. The approximate numerical strength of the church is a major problem that the church, as a unit, as in the nation, faces. The number of churches or memberships are yet to be authenticated with verification. Census taking—the enumeration of the accurate number of Nigerians—is dubious and a bewildering task. There have been arguments and nationwide squabbling, particularly in the North, where numbers are skewed. Figures given to census takers are generally accepted at face value, without the opportunity for census takers to physically see the number of persons in a household. In time, the southern states soon realized the northern states' chicanery.

Many churches did not keep consistent statistical records that could be depended on, and if they kept records, they were inaccurate or lacking factual historical data. Often, in many congregations, records were written on pieces of papers in notebooks by different well-meaning individuals who expressed varying viewpoints. The lack of an authentic central organizational system that required accurate church records defeated the need to maintain accurate information for future use. It was and has been difficult, in some instances, to know exactly where each church is located and especially where and when record keeping started.

A significantly important trend was that many individual members, not the preachers, took it upon themselves to establish churches wherever they relocated. Establishing and functioning without allegiance to an existing authoritative, hierarchical arrangement, to which the church did not subscribe, undermined the need for record keeping. At some point, evangelists who dealt with American missionaries soon realized the relevance and economic importance of church statistics, which accrued additional income. Some performed excellently among their congregations, but their data were inflated. Some of the unsubstantiated glowing accomplishments were designed to help increase financial support, especially when unscrupulous preachers knew their support came from America. Except in the northern states, that posed a unique but understandably intracultural, intractable conservatism, where supervision was more direct, consistent, and regular.

Church of Christ Restoration Movement: Its Teaching and Practice

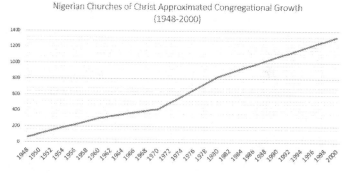

Nigerian Churches of Christ Approximated Congregational Growth (1948-2000)

Figure 32

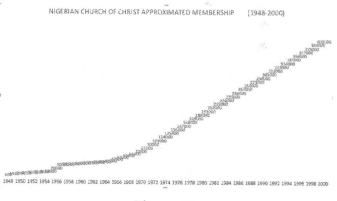

NIGERIAN CHURCH OF CHRIST APPROXIMATED MEMBERSHIP   (1948-2000)

Figure 33

Church of Christ Restoration Movement Pattern

The rise of the Church of Christ in Nigeria meant restoring the church to its primitive, simple, unadulterated biblical doctrine and practices. From the death of the last apostle, in the approximately six hundred years of silence between the Old and New Testaments, an avalanche of human-made churches emerged. Churches, beginning with the Roman Catholic Church, sprang up, purporting to teach as prophets, soothsayers, entrepreneurs, and representatives, currently as in Christ's name for God. The charlatans were a different breed and should not be confused with the hundreds who are honest, diligent groups. There have been numerous practices as different as the man-made churches, without strict adherence to biblical teachings. Through the changing course of history, God entrusted the undivided church to the hands of fallible men, whose varying agendas and focus deviated from God's plan.

I will present a broader perspective to enable readers to conduct their personal research and validate the harmony in the scriptures and the authenticity of biblical truths. We may imitate or duplicate certain aspects of perceived innovative religious practices, but we may fail to learn from each other the divine doctrinal truths, as set by God. Humans, the fallible agents, are not the authority. God of heaven and earth, the one who engineered and executed the plan of redemption through his Son and inspired apostles, is the irrefutable authority.

Digression was already in several of the first-century churches, though the divine name of the church remained intact. The conference of elders and bishops (terms are interchangeable; there is no separate function or office) was foretold of an impending departure from the faith. Paul the apostle, through the inspiration of the Holy Spirit, predicted that the return of Christ would not precede the falling away from the faith, of which "the mystery of lawlessness was already working. In view of the lawlessness, the falling away was already present and vigorously pursued, as predicted by Paul."[172] Many theorists and religionists, particularly those of the restoration movement, addressed the issue of digression in the church.

Professor F. W. Mattox emphasized that as a safeguard from digression, a close adherence to the Word of God was the only solution, just as Paul the apostle admonished the church at Ephesus. Paul told the church to take heed unto themselves and the flock, of which the Holy Spirit had made them overseers.[173] But people's egos and the desire to perennially dominate and control or to exercise authority over the weak and uninitiated, for selfish ends or personal aggrandizement, has always been a hindrance to the unity advocated by Christ. Paul wrote about Diotrephus, a prominent member, who sought preeminence among the brethren. Diotrephus, refusing to receive the apostles, used high-handed methods to control members.[174] In the second century, the growth of heresy reached an extent to which the New Testament teaching seemed to be disastrously compromised.

Cognizant of this history, the development of the providential growth of the church in Nigeria was a remarkable narrative for generations unborn. This history has had a clear message from the men and women who, through hard labor, perseverance, and bodily harm, sought to maintain and adhere to the inviolate sacred scriptures.

Like other restoration advocates, the path was clear for C. A. O. Essien, with others, who subscribed to upholding the principles and values that Christ and the apostles articulated were tenacious in upholding the truth. The issues of digression from biblical teachings, being man-made, have contributed to erroneous teachings and caused confusion and misunderstanding of church leadership roles. These issues are simplified below:

The Bible is unitary in its theme and scheme. It is a book like no other in the world. It is a book of books—sixty-six books within its volume: thirty-nine with different authors, subscribing to it during a period. Leroy Brownlow points out that it was written "during an interval of about sixteen centuries; it could not have been written accidentally."[175]

I have great wonderment in observing the authenticity of what many authors wrote, they were guided by divine inspiration. The individual authors of the Bible "lived in different periods of history, followed different occupations, labored in different customs, government and geographical locations; they lived in different times and in different sections of the world, writing independently of one another," and produced a document with a central theme that is harmoniously symmetrical. There is no book like it![176]

Calling the church by any name makes no difference by denominations if God and Christ's names are mentioned. Are we certain of this? Do we think and plan for God? No one changes our given names and calls us "doggy" to be acceptable unless we ourselves change our names and acknowledge it in a court of law. Generally, we are not referred to by appellations that were not given to us at birth or names that we did not legally change and desire to be called to be acceptable. Yet we change Christ's name or his church, his body, with designations such as the Apostolic Church, Jehovah's Witnesses, the Roman Catholic Church, the Episcopalian Church, the Methodist Church, and myriad other appellations. Paul the apostle, in his theses on the subject of division, as could be applicable to our contemporary church organizational system, appealed to us as he wrote to the Corinthians—that in the name of our Lord Jesus Christ, that all of you (Christians) agree with one another so that there be no divisions among you and that you may be united in mind and thought. (Following Paul, rhetorically I ask, is Christ divided?)

Reading through the scriptures, from Genesis through Acts, God, for reasons known to him, changed people's names, like changing Abram to Abraham.[177] Abram fell facedown, and God said to him, "As for me, this is my covenant with you: You will be the father of many nations. No longer will you be called Abram, your name will be Abraham, for I have made you a father of many nations Jacob."

Another example where God changed someone's name was when an angel asked Jacob, "What is your name?"

"Jacob," he answered.

Then the agnel said, "Your name will no longer be Jacob, but Israel because you have struggled with God and with men and have overcome."[178]

Why would God change these servants' names? That name has never changed from Israel.

Paul's name was also changed, from Saul to Paul. While they were worshipping and fasting, the Holy Spirit said, "Set apart for me Barnabas and Saul for the work to which I have called them." So, after they had fasted and prayed, they placed their hands on them and sent them off. Acts 13:9–10 reads:

> Then Saul, who was also called Paul,
> filled with the Holy Spirit, looked at
> Elymas and said, "You are a child of the

devil and an enemy of everything that is right."[179]

But we are not God, revealing the need or having the power to alter or justify changes of any name that God has given and ordained, through his infinite wisdom and pleasure.

The Bible spells out specifically the name *Christ* and his church, the body, and again what the church that belongs to Christ should wear. Having the right name, however, does not necessarily suggest one is right, without following the scriptural and acceptable pattern or acting in accordance with the teachings of the New Testament. Someone may argue that we are trifling with minutiae that have no bearing or designated name for what the church wears. The following are some examples of names scripturally described or given:

- "My church"—possessive; I will build *my church* (Matthew 16:16–20)
- Churches of Christ (Romans 16:6)
- The bride of Christ (Revelation 21:2)
- The body of Christ (Colossians 1:24)
- The church of God (1 Corinthians 1:2)
- Church of the firstborn (Hebrews 12:23)
- The church of the living God; God's household (1 Timothy 3:15)

The above names give honor to Christ and God. Man-made churches give honor to whoever establishes them. Having a scriptural name, however, does not make it acceptable or right. There are other factors to be considered. There are doctrinal issues or dogmas and tenets that govern the administration of the local church. In the governance of the local church, elders, bishops, and overseers (names used synonymously), without a hierarchical arrangement that sets one office above the other, are the ones administering the affairs of the local church. In denominations, there are layers of offices, one above the other, an arrangement forced on or established by those in authority.

The restoration movement advocates that an elder, bishop, presbyter, or overseer serve in equal capacity and that they are highly respected, without distinction. There is no top-down government.

The top-down system pays allegiance to top dictates. Churches that follow Christ without dependence on an external body, where power emanates, pay homage to Christ, their Savior. This is a complex system, and it is difficult for the human carnal mind to comprehend that any church or groups of churches could operate effectively without an earthly structure. We should wonder how churches at Corinth; Galatia; Ephesus; Philippi; the seven churches in Revelation 1:19; 2, 3, 4; and hundreds of others functioned independently without a headquarters.

The church has a scriptural foundation. It was built by Christ, and he gave his life for the body or church. That recognition is appropriated to him only, and never should it be bargained, shared, or compromised.

While with his disciples, Jesus quizzed them as to his identity. "Who do people say the Son of Man is?"

Peter responded, "Thou are the Christ the son of the living God."

Christ then told Peter, "This was not revealed to you by man, but my father in heaven." Following, Jesus said to Peter, "And I tell you that you are Peter-the pebble, little rock, *and on this rock* [Christ, the Rock] *I will build my church* [emphasis added] and the gates of Hades will not prevail against it," that is, against the Rock, which is Christ. In the dialogue between Christ, Peter and the disciples, Christ added, "Blessed are you, Simon, son of Jonah," (For what?) On the confession that you have made that I am Christ the Rock (Petros), Son of the living God. Man did not reveal the fact that I am the Christ, the Rock (Petros). Upon "this Rock," I will build my church. There was no suggestion or intimation that it would be handed over to any person, a surrogate to deputize for him on earth to rule. Again, let it be emphasized that the church belongs to Christ.[180]

The reference to Peter being given the keys of the kingdom did not empower Peter to be Christ's successor. But Peter was empowered with the keys as a symbol of authority, a spokesman, to be the first person to declare the terms of admission into the Christ's kingdom, which started on the first Pentecost after his resurrection. Christ is the authority; he is the head of the church, not any mortal being who misguides, instigates, propagates, and teaches errors. His church was started at Jerusalem, not at Rome or anywhere else as divinely preordained and geographically selected as Jerusalem.

The organizational structure of the church is biblical and in consonance with the teachings of the scriptures. The early New Testament churches were ruled by a plurality of elders, bishops, presbyters, and overseers (as mentioned, all these names were synonymous). The qualifications of the elder, bishop, or overseer were wide-ranging, covering the social, moral, ethical, and spiritual life of the candidate for the position. Unfortunately, people from most religious groups who veer from the truth seem to know more than God, and they have instituted a varying format to accommodate whoever they elect to rule over their churches.

Leroy Brownlow wrote, "Church organization is simple, but the divine plan has been greatly abused or compromised. Every attempt to improve this plan [God's plan] has resulted in apostasy and ecclesiasticism."[181]

Churches of Christ profess that admission into the kingdom is through the hearing and believing of the gospel. According to Acts 2:37–38, the people who heard Peter's preaching and the consequences for their misbehavior (sin) cried out to Peter and the other apostles, "Brethren what shall we do to be saved?"

Peter responded, "Repent and be baptized in the name of Jesus for the forgiveness of your sins, and you will receive the gift of the Holy Spirit." In these passages, the Bible defines what baptism is; that is, a burial in the water. Peter stresses the fact that baptism saves. Paul states that all those who were baptized into Christ have put on (are clothed in) Christ. Don't you know that all of us who were baptized into Christ Jesus were baptized into his death? We, therefore, were buried with him through baptism.[182] Baptism is not optional. It was not optional for Christ himself when he came to John, and John tried to dodge the issue about Christ saying, "I have need to be baptized by you and you are coming to me?" And Jesus answered, "Permit it, for thus it is appropriate for us to fulfill all righteousness" (Matthew 3:13–15).[183] Baptism by immersion is a prerequisite to salvation, and from thence, you must work and develop faith in Christ.

Churches of Christ insist that baptizing candidates in the scriptural way for the intended purpose is the right way; it is in obedience to God's purpose. God, through Christ, designed it; Christ himself complied with it. Would that be too difficult, should any person desire salvation from God?

Churches of Christ believe and teach that speaking in tongues is no longer operative. Speaking in tongues and the miraculous manifestations of healing ceased with the death of the last apostle. Reading from the scriptures, comparing how healing was performed during the apostolic times is, without question, different from what one observes among modern healers in action. All the signs made by Christ and miracles performed by the apostles were spontaneous, and only on a few occasions were the candidates required to have faith or believe. A classical demonstration of healing is Peter and John's healing the beggar by the temple gate; it had no prerequisite, no preconditions. The lame man by the gate did not ask for healing. He was a street person, a panhandler begging for money for personal needs. Some of our modern healers make fools of the innocent ones with their stunts that are prearranged with a member, who pretends or fakes illness. They spend minutes shouting in prayer for God to come down to heal, but God is not deaf—is he?

Those who allegedly speak in tongues babble indistinguishable gibberish, purported to be a tongue or language. The word *tongue*, in the scripture, is a known language or dialect that is spoken in some parts of the world by the inhabitants or anyone who has learned the language. The crowd came together in bewilderment because each one heard them speaking in his own language, *tongue*. Utterly amazed, their incredulity forced them to ask, "Are not all these men who are speaking Galileans? Then how is it that each of us hear them in his own native language?" (Acts 2:7–9).[184]

Following, in the listing of the fourteen countries that were represented, the scripture upholds the fact that "we hear them declare the wonders of God in our own tongue [language]."

Phillip's experience is a clear example of the impossibility of any disciple to extend, confer, or transfer the Spirit to another; otherwise, Phillip could have done so without having to send for Peter.[185] This meant that the gift was not transferable to a third party. However, it should be noted that there were three types of miraculous manifestations or measures of the Spirit: (1) Christ possessed the Spirit without measure; (2) there was the baptismal measure for the apostles in the household of Cornelius; and (3) there is the indwelling of the Holy Spirit, as promised by Christ. The indwelling Spirit enables believers to put to death past misdeeds because those who are led by the Spirit of God are sons of God.

Paul directly speaks of the Spirit having released us from bondage, testifying with our spirit that we are God's children. There are, therefore, differences in the function and operations of the Spirit. Each is different and should not be applied indiscriminately as having empowered anyone to speak in tongues or heal miraculously in the manner the apostles did. Miracles and tongues were for specific purposes, as described by Paul. "Love never fails. But where there are prophecies, they will cease; where there are tongues, they will be stilled" 1Corinthians 13:8-13. (The King James Version states, "Whether there are prophecies, they will fail; whether there are tongues, they will cease, and whether there be knowledge it will vanish away.") The thought did not end there; it adds, "when that which is perfect is come, then that which is in part will be done away with."[186] The New International Version rendering is, "when perfection comes, the imperfect disappears." What is, in part, incomplete refers to the old law, the Old Testament, the schoolteacher; that which is perfect when it comes (Jesus Christ); the New Testament, which James refers to as the "perfect law of liberty" or the law that is found in the scriptures, which metaphorically is intently looking to learn, to observe, and not to forget, as though looking at a mirror.[187]

There are numerous topics and issues where Christian believers have digressed from scriptures and have instituted their own form of doctrine and practices. Many have emerged in recent times, purporting to be religious but using the name of Christ for their selfish economic ventures. For many, the church has become a business enterprise for generating income for personal aggrandizement and from which those in high positions, some in mega-churches, buy expensive luxurious mansions and cars. The church is an institution, where the search to redeem humankind through the reconciliation of people to God is the ultimate divine message. One would have thought that reformation or any other means that divides Christians—if, indeed, we profess fidelity to one God—should refrain from the divisiveness among Christian people.

Coolidge Akpan O. Essien Scholarship Program

The word *memorial* is intriguing, if not self-evident, for many. There are varying connotations for families to memorialize a loved one that can be viewed as part of their grieving process. Communities memorialize a person for a life well lived, as well as one worth remembering and acknowledging. Nations, communities, and organizations have erected gigantic edifices as bastions of academic, social, and political recognition in memory of and to pay tribute to people acclaimed as famous or important. There are statues, such as the Lincoln Memorial in Washington, DC, and Dr. Nnamdi Azikiwe, Obafeme Awolowo, and Professor Eyo Ita at Calabar in Nigeria, that are reflective of the their history, struggles, and contributions to society. These monuments are never meant to be worshipped but to recognize the worth of these individuals. Libraries, colleges, and university buildings memorialize individuals who have contributed enormously to the construction of educational and research departments for the pursuit of specific academic studies. These edifices are not object of devotion, except to the uninitiated, the schizophrenics, or the ignorant ones. Scholarships are offered in memory of persons deserving recognition.

The Coolidge Akpan Okon Essien Scholarship was a memorial scholarship program designed to provide scholarships to deprived, poor children of members of the church, who could otherwise not afford to attend colleges and universities. Different forms of scholarships were considered, such as academic, merit, conditional gifts, and loan scholarships.

The academic scholarships are those that are generally awarded by local and national governments or philanthropists that may be refunded, based on criteria and conditions.

A merit scholarship is benevolent, a gift, and may not be refunded, but there is a built-in expectation that the recipient will, in time, demonstrate his appreciation or gratitude by helping the community. Another feature of the merit scholarship is that the recipient is expected to pursue values that conform with the village or organization's philosophical goals.

Loan scholarships have conditions that require the recipients to refund the amount awarded upon the completion of studies and after being gainfully employment. While contemplating these forms of awards and realizing doctrinal issues and the inabilities of young members, the board members choose to award either a merit or loan scholarship.

The inaugural meeting for the C. A. O. Essien Memorial Scholarship was held at Ukpom, Abak, on February 15, 1971. It is reproduced here with the minutes of the first meeting of the board:

> The meeting was opened with prayer, offered by Brother S. H. Ekwere at 2:30 p.m. Appointment of Officers.
>
> The following were constitutionally appointed officers of the board:

1. A. A. Isip, secretary
2. I. T. Uko, treasurer
3. E. Otoyo, chairman:

Attendance: The meeting was attended by the following members:

1. I. T. Uko
2. A B Isonguyo
3. H. Akpan
4. S. P. Ekanem
5. Edet Essien
6. W. U. Ekpo
7. Akpan Dickson
8. S. H. Ekwere
9. B. U. Ekong
10. O. U. Antia
11. E. Otoyo
12. A. A. Isip

The chairman presented orally the following topics to the board for discussion because there was no agenda:

1.   Conditions necessary for the award of scholarship
2.   Types of scholarships to be awarded.
3.   How to raise the scholarship fund
4.   How and which bank to treasure the money.
5.   How to disburse the funds

Due to financial limitations, the board agreed on the following conditions for the award of the scholarships:

1.   The child/student must come from a Christian family.
2.   The child must be a long-standing Christian himself. [In retrospect, I see gender discrimination, which perhaps was not in the minds of those who formulated the conditions. It is historic that women were not considered, as there were arguably not many of them aspiring to attend universities.]
3.   The child/student must gain admission into any of the Christian colleges.

Types of Scholarships to Be Awarded

The board agreed on two types of scholarships: namely, the loan scholarship and the free (benevolent or merit), depending upon circumstances (e.g., destitution). The chairman felt that two types of scholarships should be considered, and that the scholarship agreement committee should draft the agreement binding the recipient of the scholarship and the board. The following were immediately chosen to meet:

1. Brother S. P. Ekanem
2. Brother A. A. Isip
3. Brother Edet Essien
4. Brother O. U. Antia
5. Brother H. B. Isonguyo

Fund-Raising Scheme

Because there was no group or organization known to the board or at their disposal to legally advertise externally, churches were therefore the only available avenue to the scholarship board members. They had to consult individual members. Like Paul, who used the synagogue where people met as an opportunity to teach, local churches were auspicious and easy places, where large members met and where individual members could be approached.

Brother Isonguyo suggested that a Donation Day should be fixed in August 1970 at different locations; on that day, members who approved would willingly contribute. There was no mention of church treasury or compulsion of any person. From this moment on, the Essien Memorial Scholarship Fund was inaugurated; selected members were asked to contact churches, mostly within the then–Cross River State, to appeal for permission to use each church for oral presentations on behalf of the Scholarship Board.

Churches at Calabar, Opobo (now Ikot Abasi), Ibiono (both 1 and 2), Eket, Oron, Okobo, Eastern and Western Nsit, Uyo Central, Ikot Ekpene, and Abak all rallied supportively to embrace and to aid the program. It should be made emphatically known that individuals and not the corporate church spontaneously contributed to the support of the program. Those anti members who attacked us need to know our position was not to infringe on scriptural doctrine. For example, in Ikot-Abasi, twenty-five individual members gave small but significant amounts, based on their level of income, ranging from a few pennies to shillings and pounds. In Northern Annang, 144 individual members, who appeared like a contingent of an army, contributed the largest amount for the program, compared with other groups. Eastern Nsit, Calabar, Oron, to mention a few, were gracious in their sacrificial benevolent donation for the program.

The Essien Memorial Scholarship program awarded only a few scholarships because of the anti-movement members' virulent, rancorous attacks. They failed to realize that the program was humanitarian. It became a battleground for opposition and contentiousness. Whether right or wrong, the vocal and irrepressible attacks of the few agitators silenced the voices of the proponents of the program. To maintain peace, those who orchestrated the establishment of the scholarship program rethought the need to continue with the program under such a rancorous atmosphere. They felt it needless to further splinter an already ruptured church of the Lord.

Regardless of the inflammatory attacks and squabbling within the fold, the agitation failed to cause any visible damage or a rift in the church. Members responded with faith and temperance in moments of disagreement, and amid these, the churches joined in one purpose—to save souls. The church continued to experience remarkable growth in many parts of the country.

The graph below is illustrative of the growth pattern of the church by 2000.

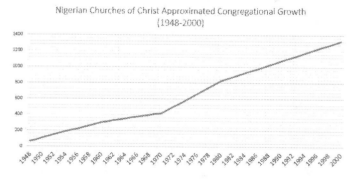

Figure 33

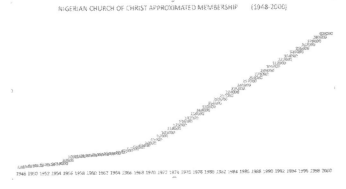

NIGERIAN CHURCH OF CHRIST APPROXIMATED MEMBERSHIP   (1948-2000)

Figure 34

Growth pattern of the church by 2000

Christian Educational Institutions

Globally, people enjoy the blessings and unique power of the media. After the invention of the printing press, ideas and thoughts were no longer restricted to privileged numbers of people but became circulated to a much wider audience who could read the same material at different locations throughout the world. From the slow woodblock printing process invented by the Chinese in AD 220 to the Gutenberg metal movable-type printing press in 1450, countless types of printing have accelerated the process of disseminating documents. Printing has served as a mirror that exposes many to scrutiny by those who are so disposed. Printing has not only served as an instrument of enlightenment, education, and entertainment but as a weapon to expose and clarify concepts, whether political, social, educational, or religious. Thus, evolved a plethora of books, magazines, tracts, and newspapers, purposely designed to educate, and inform or entertain the members, including the public, on issues that are scripturally based. Governments, where freedom of expression is sacrosanct and unrestricted, sanctioned the establishment of secular, vocational, religious institutions, and the media for the circulation of ideas. Schools that function at the behest of government recognition and approval can teach, without reprisal, courses that relate to the religious group's avowed doctrine.

It is with this view that religious schools were established by denominational groups, including the Church of Christ members. The following are a few educational institutions that Church of Christ members have established in Nigeria so far. Many of these are indigenously funded; others are funded through American churches and individual members who have oversight of the work.

The list of Christian schools below was generated in 2015 from questionnaire responses and from individuals who worked with the Christian schools. Unfortunately, there are other schools inaccessible to us and the distinctiveness of the church.

Besides providing secular education, including vocational skill instruction, the schools are unique in that they actively provide secular, moral, and religious instruction that lends itself to the value-based Church of Christ beliefs; these sections are valuable. Whether an individual is a member of the church (which is not compulsory) or not, the student is exposed to what the church believes, based on a government-approved syllabus.

Abia State Theological School, Umuahia, G. C. Iroha, 0906-442-6198. Contact the principal.

African Christian Management, Obong Ntak, Etim Ekpo, Akwa Ibom State. Contact Chief (Dr.) Moses Akpanudo.

Christian Technical College, Oyubia Town, Oron, Akwa Ibom State. Email cstcoyubia@yaho.com; contact the principal.

Christian Health Center, Mbaise, Imo State. Contact the supervisor.

Edo School of Preaching, Igara Edo. Contact the director.

Holy Land Christian College, Uhum, Ngwa, Isiala Ngwa, South LGA, Aba State. Contact the director.

Nigerian Christian Institute, Uyo, Akwa Ibom State. Contact the principal.

Nigerian Christian Bible College, Ukpom Abak, Akwa Ibom State. Contact the director/principal.

Nigerian Christian Hospital, Onicha Ngwa, Abia State. Contact the administrator.

Nigerian Institute of Arts and Theological Studies, Ntigha Onicha Ngwa State. Contact J. U. Nwachi, 0803-292-3621.

Nigerian Christian Seminary, Asa, Abia State. Contact Stephen Okoronkwo, administrator, School of Biblical Studies; Mr. Solomon Agu, Box 705, Jos, Plateau State.

School of Biblical Studies, Akwa, Anambra State. Contact the administrator.

School of Religious Studies, Port Harcourt, Rivers State.

Isiala Ngwa, South LGA, Aba, Abia State. Contact the director.

Western Nigerian Christian College, Abeokuta, Ogun State. Contact the principal.

Niger Delta Christian College of Education, Port Harcourt, Rivers State. Contact the director.

Nigerian Christian School, Nleagu Obingwa, LGA, Abia State. Nechs Education. Contact the director.

Eight Step Christian School. Contact Nkwo Ekwenye; juliuskwe@yahoocom.

Hidden Treasure, Ukwa in Aba West LGA, Abia State. Contact Uchenna-Bekee.

Osisi Christian Academy, Ukpakari, Obingwa KLG A, Abia State. Contact Oji Onyeanulam, 08034890012.

Holy Land Christian College, Uhum Mbutu Ngwa, PO Box 8, Owerrinta.

Isiala, Ngwa South, LGA Abia State. Contact Gideon Nwandire.

St. Hyacinth Christian College, Umukeogele, Isiala Ngwa South, PO Box 368, Omoba, Abia State. Contact 0703-259-7660.

Chiwe Unique Christian School, Omoba Isiala, Ngwa South LGA, Abia State. Contact the director.

SMT School, along Watchman Street, PMB 147 Abakaliki, Ebonyi State. Email Smtschool@ gmailcom; contact E. E. Offor, 0805-091-4996.

CHAPTER 9

Concluding Remarks

The reformation that engulfed Western Europe, particularly the Roman Catholic Church and the subsequent Protestant movement, spurred the splitting of Western Europe, politically and religiously. The church that was part and parcel of the social, political, economic, and religious life of the people, including the learned intellectuals and unlettered citizens, had access to the Bible and knew much about church doctrine and rituals. The growing dissatisfaction with the Roman Catholic Church did not begin with Martin Luther, as may have been thought, but with a growing population that knew of the departure from biblical tenets and doctrinal practices espoused by the apostles and the early church fathers.

Theologically, the religiosity of members on the theory of transubstantiation—the turning of bread and wine into the literal body and blood of Christ—if true, was an admission that Christians practiced cannibalism. A clearer interpretation is that the bread, representing the body of Christ, and the wine, the cup, are emblematic metaphors or representations of the body and blood of

Christ. This teaching has been debunked by theologians and scholars over the years but persists.

They witnessed the Roman Catholic Church riddled with such abuses that it could no longer be considered God's appointed custodian of Christian faith. Those who intellectualize the teaching of certain dogmas and practices that are not taught in the scriptures could not meet man's spiritual needs through their logic and imposition of erroneous views on the public. Scripture, not the decisions and traditions of men, has the final authority on any religious issue. The organizational structure of the Roman Catholic Church or any existing church in the period when the church first started (AD 33)—and for over six hundred years, including the period between the Testaments—with their pomp and pageantry, no matter how gleaming or unique, were never intended to dominate, replace, or authoritatively provide guidelines for the propagation of the gospel or salvation for man. God alone, in his infinite mercy, defines the conditions to approach him and how his earthly kingdom is to be structurally formalized for spreading the gospel—the good news.

The gap between the reformers and the Roman Catholic Church widened when Saint Augustine, an early church father, along with many proponents for change, observed that the discrepancies in the church were not in harmony with biblical teachings. The sale of indulgences was to support the construction of large edifices, but finances so collected were channeled into the pockets of cardinals, bishops, and priests. The widespread sale of church positions and the priests' avaricious holding of offices they could not adequately administer incited complaints by communicants.

The teaching and practice of indulgences, which were foisted on the people, was simply that Christ and the apostles taught members that their good works on earth had accumulated in heaven, a treasure chest, or that this act of generous-but-forced contribution shortened the individual's or a loved one's stay in purgatory, a state where the dead wait for their souls to be expatiated. Loved relatives, sons, and daughters would, like pagan ritualism, pay handsomely for the cleansing of their dead. This became a lucrative venture for the pope, priests, and the church, as they shipped enormous amounts of money to Rome from stations and countries under its realm. This unacceptable feature in the church, besides other abuses, forced Martin Luther to post his ninety-five theses.

Martin Luther (1483–1546), as a young friar, was dissatisfied with the lifestyle in the monastery. Richardson and Sullivan wrote that Luther, scourged himself, donned beggar's garb, and went out among his former fellow students with sunken cheeks and gleaming feverish eyes."[188] It was not until he received the advice of a perceptive supervisor of his monastic order that he began to read the writings of Saint Augustine and Saint Paul, where he found answers to his agonizing, lifelong quest to please God. When he read Romans 1:17, the 5. The just shall live by faith he was forced to the conclusion that the true means of salvation was not in rituals, good works, or sacraments of confirmation but to use one's reasoning power to do God's will intellectually and faithfully, and again, not in ritualistic demands on followers. True persistence and mortification is what was needed.

One of the most cultivated personalities of the period was John Calvin. He was born in France in 1509, twenty-six years after Martin Luther. As a scholar, he became a bishop at Noyon in Picardy and was converted to Protestant Christianity. Forced to flee for his life because of persecution by the Roman Catholic Church and the government of France, he was persuaded to remain in Geneva. He taught the inconceivable doctrine of predestination—that only a select number of people would enter heaven—which meant that what one did made no difference because one's salvation was guaranteed or predestined.

The agitation to return to the New Testament teaching and practices grew, engulfing people like Walter Scott, who was born in Scotland and attended the University of Edinburgh. John Wright began to organize the Baptist churches in 1801. While James O'Kelly was breaking with the Methodists, Abner Jones, as a Free Will

Baptist, reached a similar conclusion that sectarian names and human creeds should be abandoned. Unfortunately, the arguments and the logic of these men, which they deduced from the scriptures, was never heeded.

Argument and public debate were common during that era (the 1800s). Many renounced human authority to embrace the authority of the Bible, where the rule of faith and practice was described. The synod at Lexington ushered in the period in which Abner Jones started to establish churches after the New Testament order. Though his intention—and that of others who joined the movement—was genuine, after much research and study of the scriptures, they discovered missing elements in what the Bible teaches in opposition to their practices. They dissolved the structure, opting to be nothing but "Christians only." Others, like McNema, John Thompson, John Dunlavy, Robert Marshall, and David Purviance, joined James O'Kelly from their splintered groups to find authentic meeting grounds on how the church should be organized.

After a long battle and disagreement that culminated at Springfield Presbytery, there was agreement on resolutions designed to restore the New Testament Christianity. They agreed on the one Body of Christ, and the one Spirit even as we are called in one hope of our calling. The title of *reverend* ("awesome is his name") was denounced, for "there is one Lord, over God's heritage and his name is one. He sent redemption to His people. He has commanded His covenant forever. Holy and awesome is His name; King James (1611) version says, holy and reverend is His name" (Psalm 111:9–10).[189]

Coolidge A. O. Essien, after studying similar teachings from the Bible correspondence course, felt convinced that this was an irrefutable, accurate biblical rendering that held Christ's sovereignty as the head of the church. When Essien taught, many believed that Christ was the head of the church, Christ died for it, and he resurrected to save those who believe and adhere to these facts.

The teaching among the Church of Christ members is that each local congregation, actuated by the same spirit, chooses its leaders and pays its preachers appropriately—a commensurate, prevailing, decent salary. Local churches cannot and should not delegate their right to govern to any person, groups of people, or external ecclesiastical authority. However, if these independent local churches cannot pay their preachers decent salaries, they could then appeal to another congregation for financial assistance. In that case, they do not sublet their authority to govern their congregations, but upon request, churches respond generously with assistance to help meet the needs of soliciting congregations. Thus, the elders, the presbyters, or the bishops (again, synonymous titles) have oversight of each local congregation. Regarding the title *priest*, the Bible teaches that all Christian believers are "priests," without an external ecclesiastical order to appoint or ordain allegedly qualified individuals, regardless of status, to be so classified. The organizational structures set up by humankind are tantamount to a total disregard of God's will. The doctrinal practices revealed and given to humankind by God adequately sustain man through the storms of earthly and spiritual life.

> "The Spirit and the bride say, come! And let him who hears say, come! Whoever is thirsty, let him take the free gift of the water of life. I warn everyone who hears the words of the prophecy of this book: "If anyone adds anything to them, God will add to him the plagues described in this book. And if anyone takes words away from this book of prophecy, God will take away from him his share in the tree of life and in the holy city, which are described in this boo."[190] Rev, 22:18-19.

Though the Roman Catholic Church is mentioned often, it is the paragon of excellence in providing the world with a wealth of knowledge and a deluge of scholarly works. Yet as Christ wrote, "If the man should gain the whole world and lose his soul which is the bane of contention" (Mark 8: 36; Luke 9:26). Human soul is more important than humanistic materialism.

Is the Church of Christ, by its advocacy, the only one that will enter heaven? The answer is no. God is the judge, according to His will and teachings. But why take chances and not do what he says and wait for his mercy to prevail?

The Bible advances the teaching that judgment shall begin in the house of God. Members will be the first to be judged, based on his sacred writings. We will be judged according to the words that are written in the Bible.

"For if God did not spare angels when they sinned, but sent them to hell, putting them in chains of darkness to be held for judgment; if he did not spare the ancient world when he brought the flood on its ungodly people, but protected Noah, a preacher of righteousness, and seven others"[191] (2 Peter 2:4–5), how will humans respond when they stand in judgment for failure to teach and practice according to the specifications?"[192]

BIBLIOGRAPHY

1 Cor. 16:1

1 Cor. 16:1–2

1 Cor. 6:2

1 Cor. 8–9

1 Tim. 4:1–3

1 Tim. 3:1–7

1 Tim. 4:1–3

1 Tim. 4:1–2

2 Kings 2:12

2 Pet. 2:4–5

2 Thess. 2:6–7

Acts 13:1–9

Acts 17:11

Acts 2:37–38

Acts 2:6, 8

Acts 20:17–35

Acts 20:28

Acts 8

Akpan Udo, Moses, questionniare response, 2011

Anako's letter to Carson, 1962

Anako's letter to Ukpekpe, 1962

Acts 2:38

Asuquo, Etim, questionnaire response, 1985

Asuquo, Etim, and Effiong Okon Essien, response to questionnaire, 1985

Asuquo, Etim, response to questionnaire, 1985

Broom, Wendell, questionnaire response, 2003

Brother Oyo, Augustine, questionnaire response, 2013

Brother Ibra, Benedict, questionnaire response, 2008

Brother Etche, Ezekiel, questionnaire response, 2008

Brownlow, Leroy, Why I am A Member of The Church of Christ, 2002

Bryant, Patti Mattox, Divine Choreography, 2012

Bryant, Reese, *Led by His Hands,* 2011

Carson, F. F., questionnaire respponse, 1962

Carson, F F., letter, 1962

Choate, J. E., J. E., *Roll Jordan Roll: A Biography of Marshall Keeble, 2001*

Cowper, William, Songs of Faith and Praise, Howard Publishing Co., 2005

Ebong, Effiong J., Unpublished Church History, 2011

Ecc. 9:11

Ekong, George U., questionnaire response, 2013

Elangwe, Damasus Ngota, letter, 1962

Elangwe, Damasus Ngota, letter to Carson, 1965

Ephesians 1:5

Ephesians 4:9–13

Essien, Effiong Okon, questionnaire response, 1985

Farrar, Dr. Henry, questionnaire response, 1985

Galatians, 6:9–10

Goff, Reda, *The Great Nigerian Mission*, 1964

Grimley, John B. and Gordon F. Robinson, *Church Growth in Central and Southern Nigeria*

Horton, Howard, questionnaire response 1981

Isaiah 1:17–18

Isaiah 11:6

J. W. Nicks

James 1:23–25

John 4:35–36

John 5:36–40

LaVera E. Otoyo, 1963

Matt. 16:13–20

Matt. 28:19; Acts 1:5

Matt. 3:13–15

Matt. 7:7–8

Matt. 6:33

Mattox, The Eternal Kingdom, 1961

Mba, Udo Akpan Ukpong, questionnaire response, 2014

Melson

Mkpong, Ini, email questionnaire report, 2014

Mkpong, Okon E, questionnaire response, 2010

Morrison, W. W. *The Shaping of a Brotherhood, (historical Reflectonk Cheudi Pub., Plano, Texas,) 2015*

Nicks, Bill, questionnaire response, 2008

Onah, Sunday Unogwu, questionnaire response, 2008

Perry, Ralph, questionnaire response, 1985

Prof Uya, Okon Edet, *The History of Oron People, 1984*

Psalm 111:9

Rev. 22:18–19

Rev. 22:4, 19

Rev. 22:17–19

Rom. 6:14

Rom. 10:1–3

Rom. 6:1–4

Sanders, J. P., trip report, 1965

The Great Nigerian Mission, 1964

Titus 1–15

Titus 1:5

Ukpekpe, his letter to Anako, 1962

Selected Pictures, Maps, and Graphs

Maps and Other Images

Table of Graphs

Graph 3. Nigerian Churches of Christ approximate congregational growth, 1948–2000

Graph 4. Nigerian Churches of Christ approximate membership growth, 1948–2000

The above graphs are positionally and clearly identified.

ENDNOTES

PREFACE

[1] Ephesians 4:18

[2] Rom. 6:2; Col. 2:12

[3] Acts 2:38

[4] 1 Cor. 16:2

[5] Titus 1:5-9

INTRODUCTION

[6] Acts 20:28

[7] Ibid, 29

[8] 1 Tim. 3:1-3

[9] Titus 3:1-6

[10] Oyo, Augustine, Questionnaire Response, 2013

CHAPTER 1 – The Open Field

[11] Rev. 22:17-19

[12] Grimley, John B., Gordon F. Robinson, Church Growth in Central and Southern Nigeria, William B. Eerdmans Publishing Co., 1966; 11,30,127.

CHAPTER 2 - The Plea for Reason and Ecumenism

[13] Isaiah 1:17-18

[14] 1 Tim. 1-3

[15] John 5:39-40

[16] Acts 17:11

[17] John 5:41-44

[18] Couper, Williams, Songs of Faith and Praise Howard Publishing Co, Inc #26, 24

[19] Asuquo, Etim, Questionnaire Response, 1985

[20] Ibid

[21] Essien, Effiong Okon, Questionnaire Response, 2007

[22] Ibid

[23] Goff, Reda, The Great Nigerian Mission 1964, 2-3

[24] Ibid

[25] Ibid, 5

[26] Ibid

[27] Math. 7:7-8

[28] Ekong, George U. Questionnaire Response, 1963

[29] Goff, Reda, The Great Nigerian Mission 1964; 8

[30] Asuquo, Etim Questionnaire Response, 1985

[31] Ibid

[32] Martin, Glen, The Great Nigerian Mission, 1964, 41.

[33] Horton, Howard P. Questionnaire Response, 1985

[34] Ibid

[35] Ibid

[36] Ibid

[37] Ibid

[38] Ibid

[39] Ibid

[40] Ibid

[41] Ibid

[42] Ibid

[43] Ibid

[44] Goff, Reda, The Great Nigerian Mission; 1964, 23

[45] Uya, Okon Edet, A History of Oron People, 1984; 117-119

[46] Ibid

[47] Palmer, Lucien, The Great Nigerian Mission; 1964, 30

[48] Goff, Reda, The Great Nigerian Mission; 1964; 31

[49] Horton, Howard, Goff, Reda, The Great Nigerian Mission, 1964, 49

[50] Ibid

[51] Peden, Eugene, The Great Nigerian Mission, 1964,14

[52] Goff, 1964, 31

CHAPTER 4 – Foot Soldiers Movement

[53] Uya, Okon E, A History of Oron People; 14

[54] Oboho, Bassey, Unpublished History of Church of Christ Oyubia, 2013

[55] Ibid

[56] Ibid

[57] Oyo, Augustine, Questionnaire Response, 2013

[58] Nicks, J.W. Questionnaire Response, 2013

[59] Ibid

[60] Ibid

[61] Ibid

[62] Ibid

[63] Matthew 10:16

[64] Asuquo, Etim, Questionnaire Response, 1985

[65] Ibid

[66] Ibid

[67] Ibid

[68] Ibid

[69] Ibid

[70] Benedict, Ibra, Questionnaire Response, 2013

CHAPTER 5 – The Rivers State Movement (Port Harcourt – The Garden City)

[71] Ibid

[72] Ibid

[73] Ezekiel, Etche, Questionnaire Response, 2013

[74] Ibid

[75] Ibid

[76] Mba, Udo Akan Ukpong, Questionnaire Response, 2013

[77] Ibid

[78] Ibid

[79] Ibid

[80] Akpan Eka, Peter, Questionnaire Response, 2013

[81] Ibid

[82] Ibid

[83] Ibid

[84] Morrison, W.W, The Shaping of The Brotherhood; Historical Reflections, Vol.1 Cheudi Publishing Plano, Texas 2015, 47-56

CHAPTER 6 – Afro-Americans Enter/Join the Fray

[85] Ibid, 35

[86] Ibid

[87] Robinson, Edward, "Save My People from Abuse" University of Alabama, Press, 2007

[88] Hogan, R. N, Verbal conference at Figueroa Printing Press, Los Angeles, 1985

[89] Ukpekpe, T. J. O, Letter to Carson, 1962

[90] Ibid

[91] Ibid

[92] Ibid

[93] Ibid

[94] Anako, David M. Letter to Ukpekpe 1962

[95] Church and Chiefs Letter to Carson and Ukpekpe 1965

[96] Carson, Francis F. Letter to Anako/ Ukpekpe, 1/23/65

[97] Kennedy, Levi, Letter to Anako, 1965

[98] Ibid, 1962

[99] Umana, R.N, Letter to Cason, 12/28/69

[100] Elangwe, Damasus, Letter to Carson 12/28/69

[101] Ibid

[102] Ibid

[103] Carson, Francis F. Letter to Anako/ Otoyo, 4/15/64

[104] Ibid

[105] Holland, Louis/ Ruby, Letter to Carson, 1971

[106] Ibid

CHAPTER 7 – A Few Faithfull Men

[107] Etuk, Solomon U.U, Verbal Conversation, 1956

[108] Galatian 6:9-10

[109] 1 Timothy 4:1-3

[110] Titus 1:3

[111] Ibid

[112] Onah, Sunday Unogwu, Questionnaire Response, 2015

[113] Ibid

[114] Ibid

[115] Ibid

[116] Elkanah, Onwukiabo, Young, Unpublished; What You Need to Know about Unity and Peace, 1985

[117] Broom, Wendell, Questionnaire Response, 1985

[118] Ibid

[119] Ibid

[120] Ibid

[121] Bryant, Rees, Led by His Hand Second Year Trip, Feb. 1983

[122] Ibid

[123] Ibid

[124] Ibid

[125] Ibid

[126] Nicks, J.W, Questionnaire Response, 1985

[127] Ibid

[128] Farrar, Henry, Ibid

[129] Ibid

[130] Bryant, Patti, Divine Choreography 2012, Patti Mattox, 2012, 184

[131] Ibid

[132] Ibid

[133] Otoyo, LaVera E, Oral Conversation, 1963

[134] Farrar, Henry, Questionnaire Response, 2013

[135] Ibid

[136] Ibid

[137] Choat, J. E, Roll Jordan Roll, Marshall Keeble Gospel Advocate 1974, 14

[138] Ibid

[139] Ibid

[140] Ibid

[141] Ibid, 128

[142] Sanders, J.P, Into the Heart of Africa report, 1965

[143] Ibid

[144] Ibid

[145] Ibid

[146] Ibid

[147] Keesee, Dayton, Questionnaire Response, 1985

[148] Ibid

[149] Ibid

[150] Ibid

[151] Ibid

[152] Ibid

[153] Ibid

[154] Ibid

[155] Mkpong, Okon E. Questionnaire Response, 2014

[156] Mkpong, Ini, Email Questionnaire Response, 2011

[157] Perry, Ralph, Questionnaire Response, 2008

[158] Ibid

[159] Ibid

[160] Ibid

[161] John 4:34–38

[162] Ecclesiastes 9:11

[163] Akpan Udo, Moses, cited from, "Eternal Kingdom by Dr. F.W. Mattox,

[164] 2 Kings 2:11-12

[165] Isaiah 11:6

[166] Ebong, Effiong John, Unpublished History of the Church, 1985

[167] Ebong, Effiong John, Unpublished Speech

[168] Ibid

[169] Ekong, George U. Brief History of the Church speech. Questionnaire Response, 2013

CHAPTER 8 – The Rehabilitation

[170] Nicks, J.W. Questionnaire Response, 2008

[171] Ibid

[172] 2 Thess. 2:3

[173] Ibid

[174] Ibid, 7

[175] Brownlow, Leroy, Why I am a Member of the Church of
Christ, 2002

[176] Ibid

[177] Gen. 17:3–4

[178] Gen. 22:26–29

[179] Acts13:6–9

[180] Matthew 16: 13–20

[181] Brownlow, Leroy, Why I am a Member of the Church of
Christ, 2002

[182] Romans 6

[183] Matthew 3:13–15

[184] Acts 2:7–9

[185] Acts 8

[186] 1 Cor. 13:8–13

[187] James 1:2:22–25

[188] Rev 22:18–20

CHAPTER 10 – Concluding Remarks

[189] King James Rev. 22: 18–19

[190] Rev. 22:18–129

[191] 2 Peter 2:4–5

[192] Rev.22:18–19